Remarkable
Rectangles

Deceptively Simple Strip-Pieced Quilts

Robert DeCarli

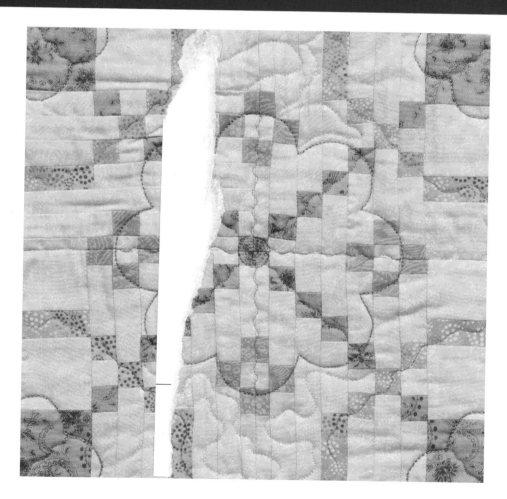

Martingale®
Create with Confidence

Dedication

To Kathleen, who has worked miracles too numerous to count and enriched my life beyond measure. She rolls on, day after day, from the beginning, loving, giving, cheering, nurturing, supporting, challenging, merging until I can't tell where she leaves off and I begin.

Remarkable Rectangles:
Deceptively Simple Strip-Pieced Quilts
© 2014 by Robert DeCarli

Martingale®
19021 120th Ave. NE, Ste. 102
Bothell, WA 98011-9511 USA
ShopMartingale.com

Printed in China

19 18 17 16 15 14   8 7 6 5 4 3 2 1

Library of Congress Cataloging-in-Publication Data is available upon request.

ISBN: 978-1-60468-355-4

Mission Statement

Dedicated to providing quality products and service to inspire creativity.

Credits

PRESIDENT AND CEO: Tom Wierzbicki

EDITOR IN CHIEF: Mary V. Green

DESIGN DIRECTOR: Paula Schlosser

MANAGING EDITOR: Karen Costello Soltys

ACQUISITIONS EDITOR: Karen M. Burns

TECHNICAL EDITOR: Nancy Mahoney

COPY EDITOR: Melissa Bryan

PRODUCTION MANAGER: Regina Girard

COVER AND INTERIOR DESIGNER: Connor Chin

PHOTOGRAPHER: Brent Kane

ILLUSTRATOR: Lisa Lauch

Contents

Introduction

"This book is about one of the greatest adventures of my life: my search for woven coverlets that I could adapt into striking, graphically interesting quilt designs. I'll soon tell you more about how I started on this unusual journey, but suffice it to say, this search became the guiding force everywhere my wife, Kathleen, and I went. We sought out fabric shops, museums, historic houses, weaving shops, country stores, and any other establishment that might possibly have any scrap of information relative to coverlets. This quest covered multiple states and involved many helpful individuals. Often, little was known of the historical provenance of these coverlets, but that didn't lessen my appreciation.

In these pages, I'll share 15 projects from among the dozens (and dozens) of quilt designs that resulted from my big adventure. These patterns give you a sample of the infinite range of possibilities for weaving-inspired quilts. And, since quilting is all about color and fabric, you'll find options in those areas, as well. For the most part, traditional woven coverlets consisted of two colors—a light and a dark (which is fine with me, as I am color-blind and it is the graphical nature I'm attracted to, not the color). Many of the featured projects continue that tradition by using a dramatic two-color design, while some of the quilts showcase a vibrant, multicolored palette. Either way, you will get a graphically stunning quilt.

Let's get started, and perhaps you'll feel inspired to embark on your own great quiltmaking adventure!"

A Cold and Wintry Day When I Was Chosen

I never thought much about epiphanies, as I never expected to experience one. If asked to describe what one might feel like, I would have said mind-shattering light or a cataclysmic event, not the dull, gray winter sky. It was a Saturday morning in February. I was standing at the window looking out into the backyard while Kathleen, my wife, cleared the breakfast dishes. It was cold, color-less, and dreary, without a leaf in sight, quiet, inside and out. There was no sign, absolutely nothing—no flash of light, no thunder, no voice, no opening of the earth or fall-ing meteor—to indicate that over the next half hour my life (and ours) would change forever.

I often wonder what I planned on doing that Saturday, but I just can't remember. Similarly, I can't remember what I did with all the time before that Saturday, but I guess that is why it's called an epiphany. I remember only looking out into the bleakness of the yard and Kathleen saying,

"I'm going to make a quilt for Robin's (our daughter's) wedding. Wanna help?"

Now, I pride myself on being less oblivious than most husbands (as well as more romantic than most, which is another story), but I had completely missed my wife's quilting phase. I remembered the decoupage phase, the macramé phase, the ceramic phase (half the basement is full of ceramic projects, which she assures me she may return to at some point in the future), the needlework phase, and the weaving phase (the loom that I surprised her with one Christmas—remember the romantic!—occupies a large part of the other half of the basement), but not the quilting phase. I had been away on some business travel over the preceding few years, but nothing extensive enough to have missed an entire phase, so I looked at her and asked, "You know how to quilt?"

I knew I was in trouble before the last word was out, but it was too late. She gave me the "I find it hard to believe that even *you* can be this oblivious" look, put the dishes down on the table, and walked firmly (she is much too ladylike and adorable to stomp) across the dining room into the living room. When I didn't budge, she stopped, turned, and gave me the look again. This time I followed as she walked upstairs, in wounded silence, and turned into the spare bedroom. I was going to point out that I hadn't been in this room since we moved into the house 14 years earlier, but didn't, as it would have only engendered the "oblivious" look. So I stood mute and penitent as she cleared the debris from a rocking chair (that I didn't even know we had), finding what at first glance appeared to be a pillowcase but was, in fact, a very small quilt. She held it up in front of her chest, which it barely covered, as tangible proof that she was a quilter.

I discreetly looked around for other quilts, but found none. Apparently, all you have to do is make one quilt, no matter how small, to be considered a quilter. Needless to say, if men were running things, only the largest quilts, the ones that involved the most blood, sweat, and tears, would really count. I pointed out to her that it was a big jump from a small wall hanging to a queen-size quilt, but she said not to worry as she had a book. Then I was going to point out that she hardly ever reads directions (as that takes all the fun out of it), but since I had nowhere to go but up, I said I'd be happy, delighted, and honored to help her make a quilt, and where do we start!

She went to the closet and selected some fabric, what looked like a green (or gray, as I am partially color-blind) piece of tag board (which turned out to be a cutting mat), and an item that looked like a pizza cutter (but was really a rotary cutter). Then she headed downstairs, motioning for me to get the old Kenmore sewing machine. When everything was set up, she said we'd make a four-patch unit, since she'd seen a picture and it looked easy and we had to start somewhere. I watched, stoically, as she cut a strip of pink and a strip of blue and sewed them together. She cut two pieces from the strips, turned one around, and went back to the machine. Less than a minute later she turned and handed me a four patch.

I stood perfectly still, looking down at the four-patch unit, with an endless number of patterns and possibilities telescoping in my mind's eye. The patterns formed in an

A Log Cabin wedding quilt

instant, morphed into other patterns, and vanished, only to reappear in a different color. I heard nothing, seeing only the patterns kaleidoscoping back and forth, in and out, around and around, and I knew in that instant what I wanted to do forever. I finally heard Kathleen calling as if from a long distance away, and reluctantly I returned. This time I paid attention as she cut some strips and explained the quarter-inch rule. I listened closely as she explained that the crosscuts had to be the same width as the original strips, otherwise you wouldn't get a square. I cut some strips, made some four patches of my own, and was hooked. I made some more and then some more and then put them together with some squares and made a king-size quilt, which I hand quilted badly. It may not be the worst first quilt ever, but it is certainly in the running. I didn't care. I loved it and couldn't wait to make another. Kathleen graciously allowed me to make the queen-size Log Cabin wedding quilt, while she made the bridesmaid dresses. After the wedding, we really got serious about quilting.

Over the next several years, I took every quilting class in sight, went to every quilt show within a hundred miles, and made quilts of all kinds. Kathleen took up appliqué and we bought fancy machines and set up a studio. I was constantly amazed at the beautiful quilts you could make using just a simple Four Patch, Nine Patch, or Log Cabin block. So simple: nothing but rectangles. I wanted to make really striking quilts, but the process was slow and I couldn't seem to come up with anything truly original using just basic rectangles. As is often the case, it happened when I wasn't even looking.

The Brandywine River Museum in Chadds Ford, Pennsylvania, allows a group of crafters to set up shop on the patio. After getting into position one cold October morning, I went down the line to say hello to the other crafters, and that is when it happened. I was visiting with the wool man when the doll lady came running in and frantically started unloading stuff from her car. I watched as she pulled out a tablecloth and spread it over the table. I noticed the intersecting circles in the design, wishing that I could do that with quilts. I continued my visiting and when I got to the doll lady, I looked closely at the tablecloth and saw that the pattern actually consisted of nothing but rectangles. Kathleen strolled by and informed me that I was looking at a classic overshot weaving pattern, which she knew because of her weaving phase. I got the camera and took 24 pictures.

I couldn't wait to get the film developed to see if I could convert the weaving pattern into a quilt, using nothing but rectangles. Well, one of us proceeded to lose the film, we didn't know the doll lady's name, it was the end of the season, and we didn't know if she would be back next year. And, I wasn't smart enough to just go to the library and borrow a weaving book. But some things are meant to be. Several months later, we were on a quilting getaway and we stopped in a little country store where I found a woven place mat with the exact same pattern.

I bought it and the fun began. I looked at the place mat and the first thing that struck me was the sense of motion: row after row of overlapping ovals, with ovals

in ovals and diagonals of squares. The second thing I noticed was that all this "motion" was created purely through the use of rectangles. That looks fairly simple, I thought. But the third thing I noticed was that the composition was more complicated than it seemed at first sight. The rows alternated—an oval in an oval, followed by an oval, followed by an oval in an oval, and so on. The next row started with just an oval, followed by an oval in an oval, followed by an oval, and so on. So, there would be no simple block that would capture the entire design. This was bad enough, but it got worse. There were three different sizes of ovals, which added to the complexity. And then there was the kicker: the designs on the inside of the ovals had the colors reversed, and, as it turned out, they were of different sizes.

It soon became clear that while this was "nothing but rectangles," it wasn't the simple but strikingly stunning grail I was seeking. I doggedly worked at translating the design into a quilt pattern, all the while hoping to find something simpler. And then I got lucky again.

At the next meeting of our quilt guild, I was telling my sad story to a few members during the break (Kathleen claims it was more like weeping and wailing than storytelling), when one of the ladies said that she had a bunch of old weaving books. Would I like to borrow them? And thus I found a coverlet from which I drafted the first weaving block (forever known to me as "the block") and my journey into the weaving world began. This one really was simple, nothing but rectangles, easy to piece, and lending itself to multiple quilt designs. As you will see, you don't even have to cut all the small rectangles.

A woven place mat similar to the one that propelled my search for coverlets

The Weaving Block

Like the Log Cabin block, the weaving block is easy to understand, simple to sew, and versatile. And, like the Log Cabin, the weaving block can be adapted to any number of variations, each yielding a whole new set of possibilities.

You can shrink the block and make place mats and table runners. You can add a curve (using rectangles only) above the first curve and form a circle in a circle. You can elongate one side and make ovals. You can remove a section from one corner and make a "window." When you put four "windows" together, you create an area for an appliqué block or a pieced block; the four-block combination turns into a frame, sort of like sashing. These variations and more are discussed in "Variations on a Theme" beginning on page 90.

This is just the beginning; the variations with the other weaving patterns are seemingly endless. The beauty of the weaving patterns is that they are all simple: just rectangles.

Fabric Preparation

I recommend that you prewash your fabric. When your fabric comes out of the dryer, press it with a steam iron. Lightly spray the fabric with spray starch before making the strip sets.

Basic Block Construction

While the basic weaving block is composed of nothing but rectangles, you don't actually have to cut rectangles. We'll use "Ezekiel's Wheel," shown on page 43, as an example. In that quilt, the weaving block consists of 11 columns and each column consists of alternating dark and light rectangles. But it all starts with making strip sets. For more details on rotary cutting strips, go to ShopMartingale.com/HowtoQuilt for free downloadable information.

1. Set your sewing machine to a shorter-than-normal stitch length (such as 2.0 mm) to prevent the seams for the cut segments from opening as you work with them.

2. Cut the number of fabric strips in the required width from each designated fabric as described in the project instructions.

3. Lay out the fabric strips in the order in which they'll be sewn. Join two strips along their long edges. Press the seam allowances in one direction. Repeat to sew the remaining strips into pairs. Then sew the pairs together to form a strip set. When sewing strip pairs together, sew from the opposite end to help avoid distortion of your strip set. (Arrows indicate stitching directions.)

4. From each strip set, cut the number of segments required in the width indicated for each column of your block.

5. Using one segment from each strip set, join the columns in numerical order (in this example, 1–11) from left to right. Press the seam allowances in one direction.

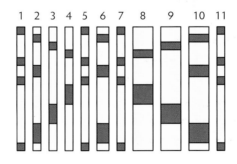

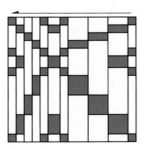

Building the Weaving Block

The basic weaving block is really most accommodating in that the columns repeat. Continuing with our example, if you cover up columns 2, 3, 4, 6, 8, 9, and 10, you'll see that columns 5, 7, and 11 are identical to column 1, so you can cut columns 5, 7, and 11 from the same strip set that you build for column 1.

Likewise, columns 2, 6, and 10 are identical except for their width, so they can be cut from the same strip set. Columns 3 and 9 are identical, as are columns 4 and 8; again, the only difference is in the width of the columns. This means that you need only four different strip-set configurations to make the weaving block in "Ezekiel's Wheel." For some of the other projects, you'll need to make different strip sets for each column in the block. However, all the projects are constructed in a similar manner: construct the strip sets, cut segments for the columns, and assemble the block.

Fabric Selection

Solids or prints that read as solids, such as batiks or mottled prints, work best for these quilts. Avoid using large-scale or multicolored prints because the weaving design could become lost.

To make the quilt, you simply rotate some of the blocks once (90°), twice (180°), or three times (270°). However, be aware that some of the blocks lose the "weaving" effect when they are rotated. The seam lines in the block are originally vertical, but when you rotate the block 90° or 270°, the seam lines become horizontal. To maintain the weaving effect, you'll need to make reversed blocks. A reverse block is constructed by simply sewing the columns in reverse order. To make the main block, sew from left to right. Sew column 1 to column 2, and then add column 3, and so on in sequential order all the way to column 11. To make the reversed block, again sew from left to right. Sew column 11 to column 10, and then add column 9, and so on until you've joined column 1. For simplicity, the instructions will refer to the main blocks as block A and the reverse blocks as block B.

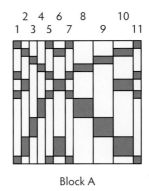

Block A

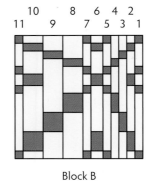

Block B

Woven Coverlet Designs Turned into Quilts

"My adventure with woven coverlets spanned several years. Throughout this entire period, I was merrily converting every coverlet I found into a quilt design. My files in Electric Quilt (the computer program I use for quilt design) were overflowing, containing more than a hundred coverlets that I had turned into quilt variations. I probably would have continued this process indefinitely had not Kathleen, my wife, observed that I now had more quilts than I knew what to do with, so I could stop. This was a fair observation, and so I decided to write a book. Of course, this created another problem—which of the hundred or so quilts should I include? Fortunately, I am a mathematician, so the solution was easy. I chose the quilts I had named for my wife, my daughter (Robin), and my two granddaughters (Charlotte and Miranda). My color-blindness necessitates Kathleen picking all the colors for my quilts, and she was particularly happy with "Indian Beadwork" (page 10), so I tossed that one in as well. I used a random number generator to select the rest. That quasi-mathematical process selected the quilts for this book. The remaining coverlet quilts wait silently and unknown in Electric Quilt, hoping to emerge at another time."

Indian Beadwork

Pieced and quilted by Bob DeCarli, Downingtown, Pennsylvania, 2012.

Quilt size: 52½" x 52½"
Block size: 12" x 12"

"This is one of the most intriguing of all the weaving patterns because when you use multiple colors, it doesn't look like a weaving at all. The weaving pattern is known as White Ball, but I am at a loss as to where that name came from. It is quite striking as a two-color pattern, but I chose to use multiple colors for the featured project. When Kathleen started playing with colors, the idea of "Indian Beadwork" just popped out. It's graphically stunning, as well as straightforward to construct."

Materials

Yardage is based on 42"-wide fabric.

2⅛ yards of green batik for blocks

1¾ yards of navy print for blocks, border, and binding

1¼ yards of red print for blocks

1 yard of turquoise print for blocks

1 yard of yellow print for blocks

3¼ yards of fabric for backing

56" x 56" piece of batting

Cutting

From the green batik, cut:

3 strips, 1¾" x 42"; cut into 6 strips, 1¾" x 21" (1 will be extra)

11 strips, 2" x 42"; cut 6 of the strips into 12 strips, 2" x 21"

2 strips, ¾" x 42"; cut into 4 strips, ¾" x 21"

2 strips, 3" x 42"; cut 1 of the strips into 2 strips, 3" x 21"

2 strips, 1¼" x 42"; cut into 4 strips, 1¼" x 21"

2 strips, 4" x 42"; cut 1 of the strips into 2 strips, 4" x 21"

1 strip, 2½" x 42"; cut into 2 strips, 2½" x 21" (1 will be extra)

1 strip, 6½" x 42"; cut into 2 strips, 6½" x 21" (1 will be extra)

1 strip, 4½" x 42"; cut into 2 strips, 4½" x 21" (1 will be extra)

2 strips, 5" x 42"; cut 1 of the strips into 2 strips, 5" x 21" (1 will be extra)

From the yellow print, cut:

14 strips, 1" x 42"; cut 7 of the strips into 14 strips, 1" x 21" (1 will be extra)

2 strips, 2½" x 42"; cut into 4 strips, 2½" x 21"

3 strips, 2" x 42"; cut into 6 strips, 2" x 21"

5 strips, ¾" x 42"; cut 2 of the strips into 4 strips, ¾" x 21" (1 will be extra)

From the red print, cut:

1 strip, 5" x 42"; cut into 2 strips, 5" x 21" (1 will be extra)

2 strips, 2" x 42"; cut 1 of the strips into 2 strips, 2" x 21" (1 will be extra)

1 strip, 6½" x 42"; cut into 2 strips, 6½" x 21" (1 will be extra)

1 strip, 4½" x 42"; cut into 2 strips, 4½" x 21"

1 strip, 2½" x 42"; cut into 2 strips, 2½" x 21"

3 strips, ¾" x 42"; cut 1 of the strips into 2 strips, ¾" x 21"

3 strips, 1¼" x 42"; cut 1 of the strips into 2 strips, 1¼" x 21"

2 strips, 1¾" x 42"; cut 1 of the strips into 2 strips, 1¾" x 21" (1 will be extra)

2 strips, 1½" x 42"; cut 1 of the strips into 2 strips, 1½" x 21" (1 will be extra)

1 strip, 3½" x 42"; cut into 2 strips, 3½" x 21" (1 will be extra)

From the turquoise print, cut:

3 strips, 2" x 42"; cut into 6 strips, 2" x 21" (1 will be extra)

1 strip, 5" x 42"; cut into 2 strips, 5" x 21" (1 will be extra)

1 strip, 4" x 42"; cut into 2 strips, 4" x 21" (1 will be extra)

1 strip, 3" x 42"; cut into 2 strips, 3" x 21" (1 will be extra)

1 strip, 6½" x 42"

1 strip, 4½" x 42"

1 strip, 2½" x 42"

From the navy print, cut:

2 strips, ¾" x 42"; cut into 4 strips, ¾" x 21" (1 will be extra)

12 strips, 1" x 42"; cut 9 of the strips into 18 strips, 1" x 21" (1 will be extra)

5 strips, 2" x 42"; cut 2 of the strips into 4 strips, 2" x 21" (1 will be extra)

13 strips, 2½" x 42"

Assembling the Blocks

"Indian Beadwork" requires eight blocks (A) and eight reverse blocks (B). Each block is made of 16 columns; the columns are simply sewn in reverse order to make the reverse blocks. We'll start by making the strip sets.

Making the Strip Sets

For this quilt, you'll make 16 strip sets, each in a different configuration. Sew the specified strips in order from left to right. Press the seam allowances in one direction.

Strip set number	Strip length	Strip width and color (N=Navy; G=Green; Y=Yellow; R=Red; T=Turquoise)									
1	21"	1¾" G	1" Y	5" R	2½" Y	2" R	1" Y	2" G	¾" N	—	—
2	21"	¾" N	2" G	2" Y	6½" R	1" Y	2" G	1" N	¾" G	—	—
3	21"	¾" G	1" N	3" G	2" Y	4½" R	1" Y	2" G	1" N	1¼" G	—
4	21"	1¼" G	1" N	4" G	2" Y	2½" R	1" Y	2" G	1" N	1¾" G	—
5	21"	1¾" G	1" N	5" G	2½" Y	2" G	1" N	2" G	¾" Y	—	—
6	21"	¾" Y	2" G	2" N	6½" G	1" N	2" G	1" Y	¾" R	—	—
7	21"	¾" R	1" Y	3" G	2" N	4½" G	1" N	2" G	1" Y	1¼" R	—
8	21"	1¼" R	1" Y	4" G	2" N	2½" G	1" N	2" G	1" Y	1¾" R	—
9	42"	¾" Y	1½" R	1" Y	5" G	2½" N	2" G	1" Y	2" R	¾" Y	—
10	42"	1¼" R	1" Y	4" G	2" N	2½" T	1" N	2" G	1" Y	1¾" R	—
11	42"	¾" R	1" Y	3" G	2" N	4½" T	1" N	2" G	1" Y	1¼" R	—
12	42"	¾" Y	2" G	2" N	6½" T	1" N	2" G	1" Y	¾" R	—	—
13	21"	1¾" G	1" N	5" T	2½" Y	2" T	1" N	2" G	¾" Y	—	—
14	21"	1¼" G	1" N	4" T	2" Y	2½" R	1" Y	2" T	1" N	1¾" G	—
15	21"	¾" G	1" N	3" T	2" Y	4½" R	1" Y	2" T	1" N	1¼" G	—
16	21"	¾" N	2" T	2" Y	3½" R	2½" Y	1½" R	1" Y	2" T	1" N	¾" G

Cutting the Columns

Cut the strip sets into segments of the specified widths to assemble the blocks. From each strip set, cut 16 segments, 8 for block A and 8 for block B.

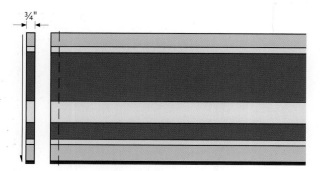

Strip set 1.
Cut 16 segments, ¾" wide, for column 1.

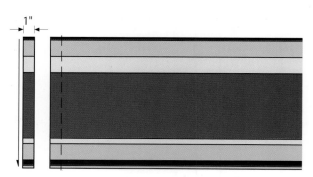

Strip set 2.
Cut 16 segments, 1" wide, for column 2.

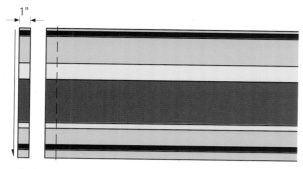

Strip set 3.
Cut 16 segments, 1" wide, for column 3.

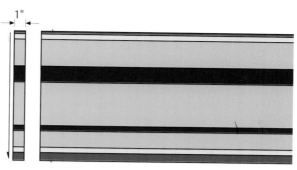

Strip set 7.
Cut 16 segments, 1" wide, for column 7.

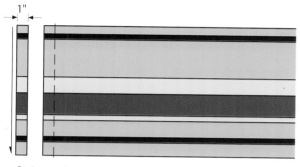

Strip set 4.
Cut 16 segments, 1" wide, for column 4.

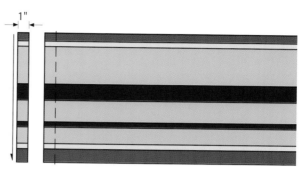

Strip set 8.
Cut 16 segments, 1" wide, for column 8.

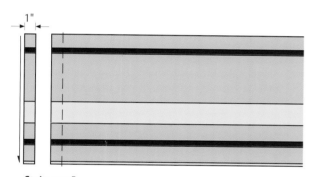

Strip set 5.
Cut 16 segments, 1" wide, for column 5.

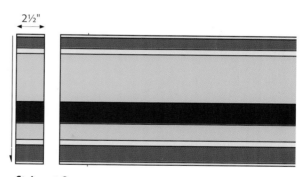

Strip set 9.
Cut 16 segments, 2½" wide, for column 9.

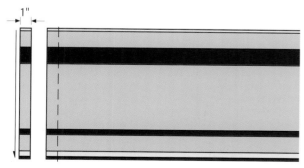

Strip set 6.
Cut 16 segments, 1" wide, for column 6.

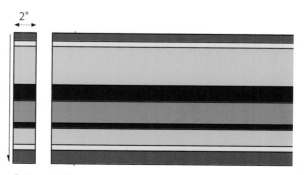

Strip set 10.
Cut 16 segments, 2" wide, for column 10.

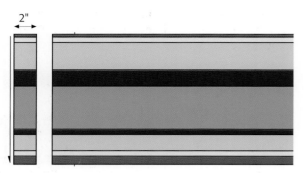

Strip set 11.
Cut 16 segments, 2" wide, for column 11.

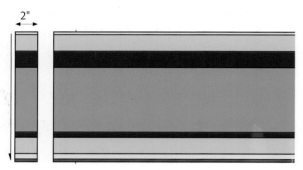

Strip set 12.
Cut 16 segments, 2" wide, for column 12.

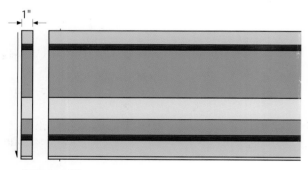

Strip set 13.
Cut 16 segments, 1" wide, for column 13.

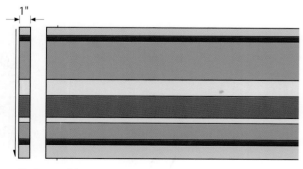

Strip set 14.
Cut 16 segments, 1" wide, for column 14.

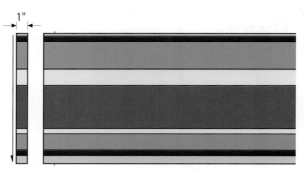

Strip set 15.
Cut 16 segments, 1" wide, for column 15.

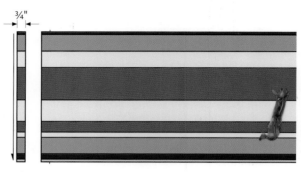

Strip set 16.
Cut 16 segments, ¾" wide, for column 16.

Completing the Blocks

1. Using one segment from each strip set as described, make eight A blocks, sewing the columns in numerical order 1–16 from left to right. Press the seam allowances in one direction as shown.

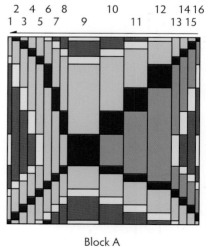

Block A
Make 8.

2. Using one segment from each strip set, make eight B blocks by sewing the columns in reverse order 16–1 from left to right. Press the seam allowances in one direction as shown.

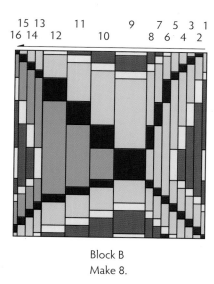

15 13   11   9   7 5 3 1
16 14   12   10   8 6 4 2

Block B
Make 8.

toward the border. Sew the 52½"-long strips to the top and bottom of the quilt top. Press the seam allowances toward the border.

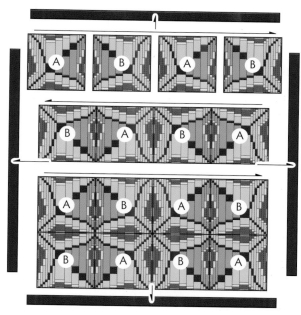

Quilt assembly

Assembling the Quilt

1. Arrange the blocks as shown in the quilt assembly diagram above right. Note that some of the blocks are rotated 180° to form the quilt pattern.

2. Once your blocks are all arranged, sew them together in rows, pressing the seam allowances in opposite directions from row to row. Then sew the rows together and press the seam allowances in one direction. The quilt-top center should measure 48½" square.

3. Join six of the navy 2½"-wide strips end to end. From the pieced strip, cut two 48½"-long strips and two 52½"-long strips. Sew the 48½"-long strips to opposite sides of the quilt top. Press the seam allowances

Finishing the Quilt

For details on any of the following steps, go to ShopMartingale.com/HowtoQuilt for free downloadable information.

1. Cut and piece the backing fabric and then layer the quilt top with batting and backing.

2. After basting the layers together, hand or machine quilt as desired. Trim the batting and backing so that the edges are even with the quilt top.

3. Using the remaining navy 2½"-wide strips, make and attach binding.

Sunny South

Pieced and quilted by Pat Smith, Downingtown, Pennsylvania, 2012.

Quilt size: 24½" x 24½"
Block size: 5" x 5"

"The first woven coverlet that I serendipitously stumbled across became the design inspiration for "Ezekiel's Wheel," shown on page 43, and I had no idea as to what else was out there. I searched far and wide for weaving designs, and soon a pattern emerged. There seemed to be two types of woven coverlets: stars and circles. There was some variation, but basically the circular-patterned coverlets had diamonds or squares at their intersection (as in "Ezekiel's Wheel" or "Thirteen States" on page 68). The design shown in "Sunny South" is just different enough, however, to make it interesting. It has a sort of keyhole effect between blocks and an X forms in the center where the blocks are joined. In addition, the block is small—just 5"—making it ideal for place mats and table runners. "

Materials

Yardage is based on 42"-wide fabric.

1 yard of orange print for blocks, border, and binding
1 yard of yellow print for blocks
⅓ yard of pink print for blocks
⅛ yard of lime-green print for blocks
1 yard of fabric for backing
29" x 29" piece of batting

Cutting

From the pink print, cut:

1 strip, ¾" x 42"; cut into 2 strips, ¾" x 21"
3 strips, 1" x 42"; cut into 6 strips, 1" x 21" (1 will be extra)
1 strip, 2" x 42"

From the yellow print, cut:

4 strips, 2" x 42"; cut *3 of the strips* into 6 strips, 2" x 21"
2 strips, 1" x 42"; cut into 4 strips, 1" x 21" (1 will be extra)
2 strips, 2¼" x 42"; cut into 4 strips, 2¼" x 21" (1 will be extra)
3 strips, ¾" x 42"; cut *2 of the strips* into 4 strips, ¾" x 21" (1 will be extra)
1 strip, 2¾" x 42"; cut into 2 strips, 2¾" x 21"
1 strip, 1¼" x 42"; cut into 2 strips, 1¼" x 21"
2 strips, 1¾" x 42"; cut *1 of the strips* into 2 strips, 1¾" x 21" (1 will be extra)
1 strip, 4" x 42"; cut into 2 strips, 4" x 21" (1 will be extra)

From the lime-green print, cut:

2 strips, 1" x 42"; cut into 4 strips, 1" x 21"
1 strip, ¾" x 42"; cut into 2 strips, ¾" x 21"

From the orange print, cut:

1 strip, ¾" x 42"; cut into 2 strips, ¾" x 21" (1 will be extra)
1 strip, 2" x 42"; cut into 2 strips, 2" x 21" (1 will be extra)
3 strips, 1" x 42"; cut *2 of the strips* into 4 strips, 1" x 21"
2 strips, 2½" x 20½"
2 strips, 2½" x 24½"
3 strips, 2½" x 42"

Assembling the Blocks

"Sunny South" requires eight blocks (A) and eight reverse blocks (B). Each block is made of nine columns; the columns are simply sewn in reverse order to make the reverse blocks. We'll start by making the strip sets.

Making the Strip Sets

For this quilt, you'll make nine strip sets, each in a different configuration as shown on pages 18 and 19. Sew the specified strips in order from left to right. Press the seam allowances in one direction.

Strip set number	Strip length	Strip width and color (P=Pink; O=Orange; Y=Yellow; L=Lime green)					
1	21"	¾" P	2" Y	1" L	1" Y	1" L	2¼" Y
2	21"	¾" Y	1" P	2" Y	1" L	2¾" Y	—
3	21"	1¼" Y	1" P	4" Y	¾" O	—	—
4	21"	1¾" Y	1" P	2" Y	2" O	¾" Y	—
5	21"	¾" L	2" Y	1" P	1" Y	1" O	2¼" Y
6	21"	¾" Y	1" L	2" Y	1" O	2 ¾" Y	—
7	21"	¾" L	2" Y	1" O	1" Y	1" P	2¼" Y
8	42"	1¾" Y	1" O	2" Y	2" P	¾" Y	—
9	21"	1¼" Y	1" O	4" Y	¾" P	—	—

Cutting the Columns

Cut the strip sets into segments of the specified widths to assemble the blocks. The segment width varies for each strip set, as indicated below. From each strip set, cut 16 segments, 8 for block A and 8 for block B.

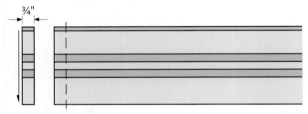

Strip set 1.
Cut 16 segments, ¾" wide, for column 1.

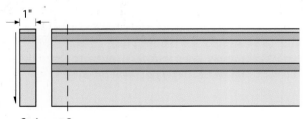

Strip set 2.
Cut 16 segments, 1" wide, for column 2.

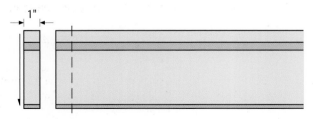

Strip set 3.
Cut 16 segments, 1" wide, for column 3.

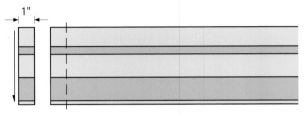

Strip set 4.
Cut 16 segments, 1" wide, for column 4.

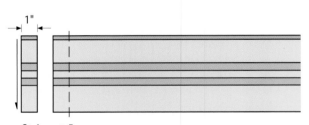

Strip set 5.
Cut 16 segments, 1" wide, for column 5.

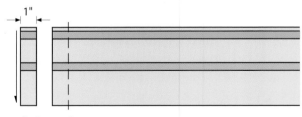

Strip set 6.
Cut 16 segments, 1" wide, for column 6.

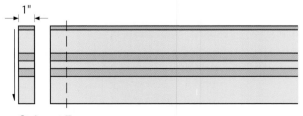

Strip set 7.
Cut 16 segments, 1" wide, for column 7.

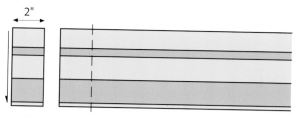

Strip set 8.
Cut 16 segments, 2" wide, for column 8.

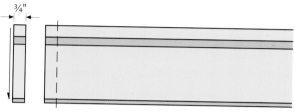

Strip set 9.
Cut 16 segments, ¾" wide, for column 9.

Completing the Blocks

1. Using one segment from each strip set as described, make eight A blocks, sewing the columns in numerical order 1–9 from left to right. Press the seam allowances in one direction as shown.

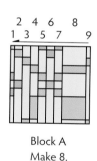

Block A
Make 8.

2. Using one segment from each strip set, make eight B blocks by sewing the columns in reverse order 9–1 from left to right. Press the seam allowances in one direction as shown.

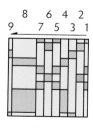

Block B
Make 8.

Assembling the Quilt

1. Arrange the blocks as shown in the quilt assembly diagram below. Note that some of the blocks are rotated 180° to form the quilt pattern.

2. Once your blocks are all arranged, sew them together in rows, pressing the seam allowances in opposite directions from row to row. Then sew the rows together and press the seam allowances in one direction. The quilt-top center should measure 20½" square.

3. Sew the orange 20½"-long strips to opposite sides of the quilt top. Press the seam allowances toward the border. Sew the orange 24½"-long strips to the top and bottom of the quilt top. Press the seam allowances toward the border.

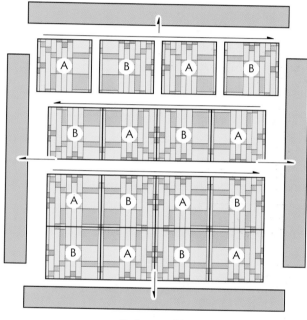

Quilt assembly

Finishing the Quilt

For details on any of the following steps, go to ShopMartingale.com/HowtoQuilt for free downloadable information.

1. Cut and piece the backing fabric and then layer the quilt top with batting and backing.

2. After basting the layers together, hand or machine quilt as desired. Trim the batting and backing so that the edges are even with the quilt top.

3. Using the orange 2½" x 42" strips, make and attach binding.

Wedding Ring

Pieced and quilted by Ellen McMillen, Downingtown, Pennsylvania, 2012.

Quilt size: 32½" x 32½"
Block size: 7" x 7"

For those of you who don't appliqué and run for the hills at the thought of curved piecing, this quilt is for you. It's every bit as spectacular as the traditional Double Wedding Ring quilt and uses nothing but strip sets to construct. By interchanging the blue and the pink in half the blocks, you get a quilt for both genders!

Materials

Yardage is based on 42"-wide fabric.

2 yards of blue print for blocks, border, and binding

1⅜ yards of pink print for blocks

1⅛ yards of fabric for backing

36" x 36" piece of batting

Cutting

From the blue print, cut:

3 strips, ¾" x 42"; cut into 6 strips, ¾" x 21"

10 strips, 1" x 42"; cut into 20 strips, 1" x 21" (1 will be extra)

4 strips, 1¼" x 42"; cut into 8 strips, 1¼" x 21" (1 will be extra)

2 strips, 1½" x 42"; cut into 4 strips, 1½" x 21" (1 will be extra)

2 strips, 1¾" x 42"; cut into 4 strips, 1¾" x 21"

1 strip, 3¼" x 42"; cut into 2 strips, 3¼" x 21"

1 strip, 3¾" x 42"; cut into 2 strips, 3¾" x 21" (1 will be extra)

2 strips, 2" x 42"; cut into 4 strips, 2" x 21" (1 will be extra)

1 strip, 3" x 42"; cut into 2 strips, 3" x 21" (1 will be extra)

1 strip, 2¼" x 42"; cut into 2 strips, 2¼" x 21"

1 strip, 2¾" x 42"; cut into 2 strips, 2¾" x 21"

2 strips, 2½" x 28½"

2 strips, 2½" x 32½"

4 strips, 2½" x 42"

From the pink print, cut:

4 strips, ¾" x 42"; cut into 8 strips, ¾" x 21" (1 will be extra)

10 strips, 1" x 42"; cut into 20 strips, 1" x 21" (1 will be extra)

4 strips, 1¼" x 42"; cut into 8 strips, 1¼" x 21"

2 strips, 1½" x 42"; cut into 4 strips, 1½" x 21" (1 will be extra)

2 strips, 1¾" x 42"; cut into 4 strips, 1¾" x 21"

1 strip, 3¼" x 42"; cut into 2 strips, 3¼" x 21"

1 strip, 3¾" x 42"; cut into 2 strips, 3¾" x 21" (1 will be extra)

2 strips, 2" x 42"; cut into 4 strips, 2" x 21" (1 will be extra)

1 strip, 3" x 42"; cut into 2 strips, 3" x 21" (1 will be extra)

1 strip, 2¼" x 42"; cut into 2 strips, 2¼" x 21"

1 strip, 2¾" x 42"; cut into 2 strips, 2¾" x 21"

Assembling the Blocks

For the pink sections, you'll need four blocks (A) and four reversed blocks (B). For the blue sections, you'll need four blocks (C) and four reversed blocks (D). Each block is made of 14 columns; the columns are simply sewn in reverse order to make the reverse blocks. We'll start by making the strip sets.

Making the Strip Sets

For this quilt, you'll make seven different strip-set configurations (1–7) for blocks A and B and seven different strip-set configurations (8–14) for blocks C and D as shown on pages 22–24. Sew the specified strips in order from left to right. Press the seam allowances in one direction.

Strip set number	Strip length	Strip width and color (B=Blue; P=Pink)								
1	21"	¾" B	3¼" P	1" B	3¾" P	¾" B	—	—	—	—
2	21"	¾" P	1" B	2" P	1¼" B	3¼" P	1½" B	¾" P	—	—
3	21"	1¼" P	1" B	1" P	1" B	3" P	1½" B	1" P	1" B	¾" P
4	21"	1¾" P	1" B	2¼" P	1¾" B	1½" P	1" B	1¼" P	—	—
5	21"	1¼" P	1" B	1" P	1" B	1¼" P	1" B	2¾" P	1" B	1¼" P
6	21"	¾" P	1" B	2" P	1¼" B	2¾" P	1" B	1¾" P	—	—
7	21"	¾" B	2" P	1" B	1¼" P	1" B	2¼" P	1" B	1¾" P	—
8	21"	¾" P	3¼" B	1" P	3¾" B	¾" P	—	—	—	—
9	21"	¾"B	1" P	2" B	1¼" P	3¼" B	1½" P	¾" B	—	—
10	21"	1¼" B	1" P	1" B	1" P	3" B	1½" P	1" B	1" P	¾" B
11	21"	1¾" B	1" P	2¼" B	1¾" P	1½" B	1" P	1¼" B	—	—
12	21"	1¼" B	1" P	1" B	1" P	1¼"B	1" P	2¾" B	1" P	1¼" B
13	21"	¾" B	1" P	2" B	1¼" P	2¾" B	1" P	1¾" B	—	—
14	21"	¾" P	2" B	1" P	1¼" B	1" P	2¼" B	1" P	1¾" B	—

Cutting the Columns

Cut the strip sets into the specified widths and quantities to assemble blocks A, B, C, and D. The segment width varies for each strip set, as indicated below.

Strip set 1.
Cut 4 segments, ¾" wide, for block A column 1.
Cut 4 segments, ¾" wide, for block A column 14.
Cut 4 segments, ¾" wide, for block B column 1.
Cut 4 segments, ¾" wide, for block B column 14.

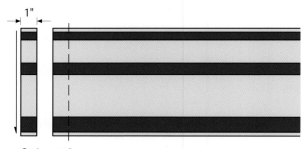

Strip set 2.
Cut 4 segments, 1" wide, for block A column 2.
Cut 4 segments, 1" wide, for block A column 13
  (rotate the segments 180°).
Cut 4 segments, 1" wide, for block B column 2.
Cut 4 segments, 1" wide, for block B column 13
  (rotate the segments 180°).

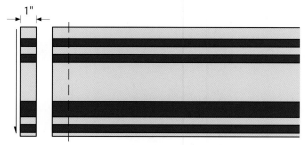

Strip set 3.
Cut 4 segments, 1" wide, for block A column 3.
Cut 4 segments, 1" wide, for block A column 12
  (rotate the segments 180°).
Cut 4 segments, 1" wide, for block B column 3.
Cut 4 segments, 1" wide, for block B column 12
  (rotate the segments 180°).

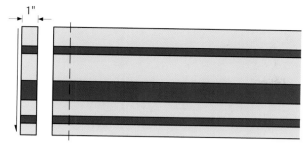

Strip set 4.
Cut 4 segments, 1" wide, for block A column 4.
Cut 4 segments, 1" wide, for block A column 11
  (rotate the segments 180°).
Cut 4 segments, 1" wide, for block B column 4.
Cut 4 segments, 1" wide, for block B column 11
  (rotate the segments 180°).

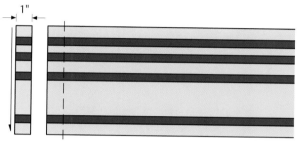

Strip set 5.
Cut 4 segments, 1" wide, for block A column 5.
Cut 4 segments, 1" wide, for block A column 10
  (rotate the segments 180°).
Cut 4 segments, 1" wide, for block B column 5.
Cut 4 segments, 1" wide, for block B column 10
  (rotate the segments 180°).

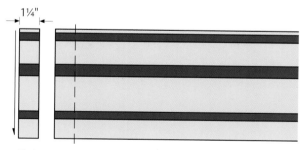

Strip set 6.
Cut 4 segments, 1¼" wide, for block A column 6.
Cut 4 segments, 1¼" wide, for block A column 9
  (rotate the segments 180°).
Cut 4 segments, 1¼" wide, for block B column 6.
Cut 4 segments, 1¼" wide, for block B column 9
  (rotate the segments 180°).

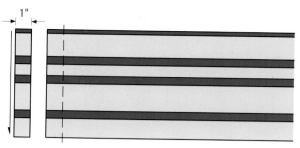

Strip set 7.
Cut 4 segments, 1" wide, for block A column 7.
Cut 4 segments, 1" wide, for block A column 8
  (rotate the segments 180°).
Cut 4 segments, 1" wide, for block B column 7.
Cut 4 segments, 1" wide, for block B column 8
  (rotate the segments 180°).

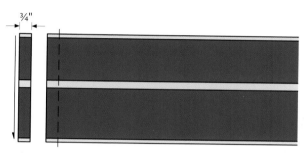

Strip set 8.
Cut 4 segments, ¾" wide, for block C column 1.
Cut 4 segments, ¾" wide, for block C column 14
  (rotate the segments 180°).
Cut 4 segments, ¾" wide, for block D column 1.
Cut 4 segments, ¾" wide, for block D column 14
  (rotate the segments 180°).

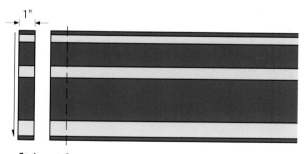

Strip set 9.
Cut 4 segments, 1" wide, for block C column 2.
Cut 4 segments, 1" wide, for block C column 13
  (rotate the segments 180°).
Cut 4 segments, 1" wide, for block D column 2.
Cut 4 segments, 1" wide, for block D column 13
  (rotate the segments 180°).

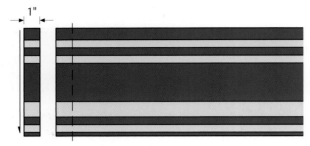

Strip set 10.
Cut 4 segments, 1" wide, for block C column 3.
Cut 4 segments, 1" wide, for block C column 12
  (rotate the segments 180°).
Cut 4 segments, 1" wide, for block D column 3.
Cut 4 segments, 1" wide, for block D column 12
  (rotate the segments 180°).

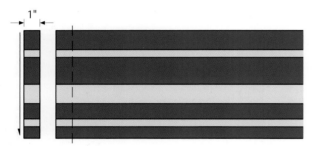

Strip set 11.
Cut 4 segments, 1" wide, for block C column 4.
Cut 4 segments, 1" wide, for block C column 11
  (rotate the segments 180°).
Cut 4 segments, 1" wide, for block D column 4.
Cut 4 segments, 1" wide, for block D column 11
  (rotate the segments 180°).

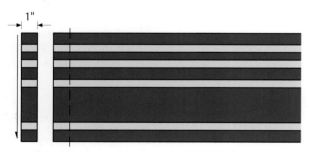

Strip set 12.
Cut 4 segments, 1" wide, for block C column 5.
Cut 4 segments, 1" wide, for block C column 10
  (rotate the segments 180°).
Cut 4 segments, 1" wide, for block D column 5.
Cut 4 segments, 1" wide, for block D column 10
  (rotate the segments 180°).

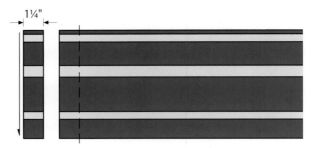

Strip set 13.
Cut 4 segments, 1¼" wide, for block C column 6.
Cut 4 segments, 1¼" wide, for block C column 9
  (rotate the segments 180°).
Cut 4 segments, 1¼" wide, for block D column 6.
Cut 4 segments, 1¼" wide, for block D column 9
  (rotate the segments 180°).

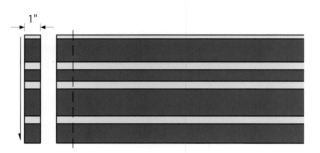

Strip set 14.
Cut 4 segments, 1" wide, for block C column 7.
Cut 4 segments, 1" wide, for block C column 8
  (rotate the segments 180°).
Cut 4 segments, 1" wide, for block D column 7.
Cut 4 segments, 1" wide, for block D column 8
  (rotate the segments 180°).

Completing the Blocks

1. Using the segments from strip sets 1–7 as described, make four A blocks, sewing the columns in numerical order 1–14 from left to right. Press the seam allowances in one direction as shown.

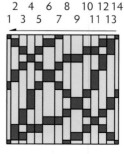

Block A
Make 4.

2. Using the segments from strip sets 1–7 as described, make four B blocks by sewing the columns in reverse order 14–1 from left to right. Press the seam allowances in one direction as shown.

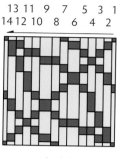

13 11 9 7 5 3 1
14 12 10 8 6 4 2

Block B
Make 4.

3. Using the segments from strip sets 8–14 as described, make four C blocks, sewing the columns in numerical order 1–14 from left to right. Press the seam allowances in one direction as shown.

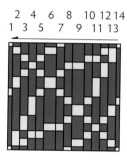

2 4 6 8 10 12 14
1 3 5 7 9 11 13

Block C
Make 4.

4. Using the segments from strip sets 8–14 as described, make four D blocks by sewing the columns in reverse order 14–1 from left to right. Press the seam allowances in one direction as shown.

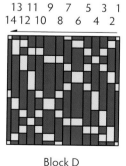

13 11 9 7 5 3 1
14 12 10 8 6 4 2

Block D
Make 4.

Assembling the Quilt

1. Arrange the blocks as shown in the quilt assembly diagram below. Note that some of the blocks are rotated 180° to form the quilt pattern.

2. Once your blocks are all arranged, sew them together in rows, pressing the seam allowances in opposite directions from row to row. Then sew the rows together and press the seam allowances in one direction. The quilt-top center should measure 28½" square.

3. Sew the blue 28½"-long strips to opposite sides of the quilt top. Press the seam allowances toward the border. Sew the blue 32½"-long strips to the top and bottom of the quilt top. Press the seam allowances toward the border.

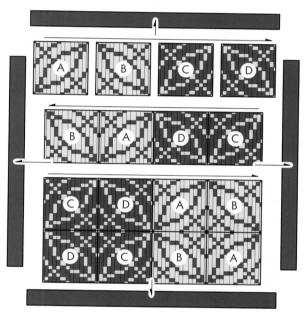

Quilt assembly

Finishing the Quilt

For details on any of the following steps, go to ShopMartingale.com/HowtoQuilt for free downloadable information.

1. Cut and piece the backing fabric and then layer the quilt top with batting and backing.

2. After basting the layers together, hand or machine quilt as desired. Trim the batting and backing so that the edges are even with the quilt top.

3. Using the blue 2½" x 42" strips, make and attach binding.

Ludwig's Corner

Pieced by Kathleen DeCarli, Downingtown, Pennsylvania, 2012. Quilted by Kim Loar, Lancaster, Pennsylvania.

Quilt size: 92½" x 92½"
Block size: 8" x 8"

As I searched far and wide for woven coverlets, I found enough coverlets to fill at least two books, but I didn't find many of the creators. Most of the coverlets were made anonymously, with no surviving information about their heritage. "Ludwig's Corner" was one of the few exceptions, but even here, the data was more tantalizing than informative. The reference said only "Johann Ludwig Speck's No 20." Wouldn't you just love to see 1 to 19? And were there any more after 20? If I could only have one of Johann's coverlets, I like to think that this one is probably the best. It is the classic circle-square, but with a twist. The square part has little loops surrounding the circle, creating a circle-in-a-circle effect. My wife, Kathleen, took one look at this design and said it had to be made into a bed quilt in blue and white.

Materials

Yardage is based on 42"-wide fabric.

8½ yards of white-on-white print for blocks
5¾ yards of blue print for blocks and border
¾ yard of blue stripe for binding
8½ yards of fabric for backing
96" x 96" piece of batting

Cutting

From the blue print, cut:

26 strips, 1½" x 42"
64 strips, 1" x 42"
10 strips, 2" x 42"
9 strips, 6½" x 42"

From the white-on-white print, cut:

26 strips, 2" x 42"
26 strips, 1½" x 42"
8 strips, 4" x 42"
18 strips, 4½" x 42"
20 strips, 1" x 42"
20 strips, 2½" x 42"

From the blue stripe, cut:

2½"-wide bias binding strips to total 380"

Assembling the Blocks

"Ludwig's Corner" requires 26 blocks (A) and 26 reverse blocks (B). You'll also need 24 blocks (C) and 24 reverse blocks (D). Each block is made of 11 columns; the columns are simply sewn in reverse order to make the reverse blocks. We'll start by making four different types of strip sets to make all of the blocks.

> ### Versatile Blocks
>
> "Ludwig's Corner" is one of the most versatile of the weaving-inspired quilts. If you use just the A and B blocks, you get the tradition wheel design and some other intriguing geometric configurations. But it's the C and D blocks that are most impressive and make a completely unique quilt which is shown in "Variations on a Theme" on page 90. It looks nothing like "Ludwig's Corner" or any of the other quilts.

Making the Strip Sets

For this quilt, you'll use four different strip-set configurations as shown on page 28. Sew the specified strips in numerical order from left to right. Press the seam allowances in one direction. Make eight *each* of strip sets 1 and 2. Make 10 *each* of strip sets 3 and 4.

Strip set number	Strip length	Strip width and color (B=Blue; W=White)						
1	42"	1½" B	2" W	1" B	1½" W	1" B	4" W	—
2	42"	1½" W	1" B	2" W	1½" B	4½" W	—	—
3	42"	2" W	1" B	4½" W	1" B	1" W	1½" B	—
4	42"	2½" W	1" B	2½" W	2" B	1" W	1" B	1½" W

Cutting the Columns

Cut the strip sets into segments of the specified widths and quantities to assemble blocks A, B, C, and D. The segment width varies for each strip set, as indicated.

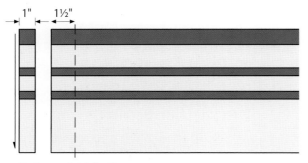

Strip set 1. Make 8.
Cut 52 segments, 1½" wide, for column 1
 (26 for block A and 26 for block B).
Cut 52 segments, 1" wide, for column 5
 (26 for block A and 26 for block B).
Cut 52 segments, 1" wide, for column 7
 (26 for block A and 26 for block B).
Cut 48 segments, 1" wide, for column 2
 (24 for block C and 24 for block D).
Cut 48 segments, 1½" wide, for column 6
 (24 for block C and 24 for block D).

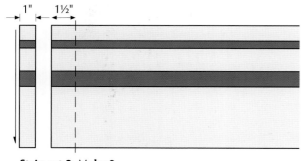

Strip set 2. Make 8.
Cut 52 segments, 1" wide, for column 2
 (26 for block A and 26 for block B).
Cut 52 segments, 1½" wide, for column 6
 (26 for block A and 26 for block B).
Cut 48 segments, 1½" wide, for column 1
 (24 for block C and 24 for block D).
Cut 48 segments, 1" wide, for column 5
 (24 for block C and 24 for block D).
Cut 48 segments, 1" wide, for column 7
 (24 for block C and 24 for block D).

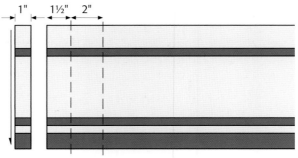

Strip set 3. Make 10.
Cut 52 segments, 1" wide, for column 3
 (26 for block A and 26 for block B).
Cut 52 segments, 1" wide, for column 9
 (26 for block A and 26 for block B).
Cut 52 segments, 1½" wide, for column 11
 (26 for block A and 26 for block B).
Cut 48 segments, 1" wide, for column 4
 (24 for block C and 24 for block D).
Cut 48 segments, 2" wide, for column 8
 (24 for block C and 24 for block D).
Cut 48 segments, 1" wide, for column 10
 (24 for block C and 24 for block D).

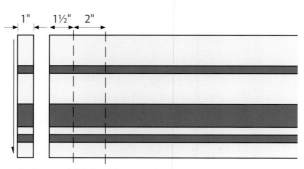

Strip set 4. Make 10.
Cut 52 segments, 1" wide, for column 4
 (26 for block A and 26 for block B).
Cut 52 segments, 2" wide, for column 8
 (26 for block A and 26 for block B).
Cut 52 segments, 1" wide, for column 10
 (26 for block A and 26 for block B).
Cut 48 segments, 1" wide, for column 3
 (24 for block C and 24 for block D).
Cut 48 segments, 1" wide, for column 9
 (24 for block C and 24 for block D).
Cut 48 segments, 1½" wide, for column 11
 (24 for block C and 24 for block D).

Completing the Blocks

1. Using the segments from each strip set as described, make 26 A blocks, sewing the columns in numerical order 1–11 from left to right. Press the seam allowances in one direction as shown.

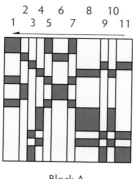

Block A
Make 26.

2. Using the segments from each strip set as described, make 26 B blocks by sewing the columns in reverse order 11–1 from left to right. Press the seam allowances in one direction as shown.

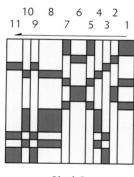

Block B
Make 26.

3. Using the segments from each strip set as described, make 24 C blocks, sewing the columns in numerical order 1–11 from left to right. Press the seam allowances in one direction as shown.

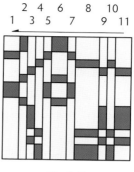

Block C
Make 24.

4. Using the segments from each strip set as described, make 24 D blocks by sewing the columns in reverse order 11–1 from left to right. Press the seam allowances in one direction as shown.

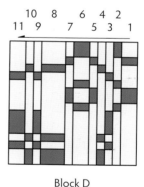

Block D
Make 24.

Assembling the Quilt

1. Arrange the blocks as shown in the quilt assembly diagram on page 30. Note that some of the blocks are rotated 180° to form the quilt pattern.

2. Once your blocks are all arranged, sew them together in rows, pressing the seam allowances in opposite directions from row to row. Then sew the rows together and press the seam allowances in one direction. The quilt-top center should measure 80½" square.

3. Join the blue 6½"-wide strips end to end. From the pieced strip, cut two 80½"-long strips and two 92½"-long strips. Sew the 80½"-long strips to opposite sides of the quilt top. Press the seam allowances toward the border. Sew the 92½"-long strips to the top and bottom of the quilt top. Press the seam allowances toward the border.

Finishing the Quilt

For details on any of the following steps, go to ShopMartingale.com/HowtoQuilt for free downloadable information.

1. Cut and piece the backing fabric and then layer the quilt top with batting and backing.

2. After basting the layers together, hand or machine quilt as desired. Trim the batting and backing so that the edges are even with the quilt top.

3. Using the blue-striped 2½"-wide bias strips, make and attach binding.

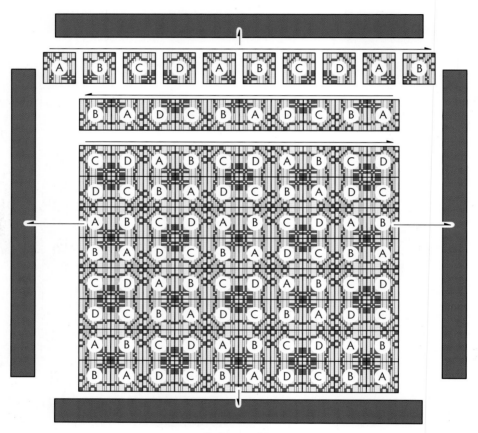

Quilt assembly

Chinese Screen

Pieced by Pat Sherman, Lancaster, Pennsylvania, 2012. Quilted by Kim Loar, Lancaster, Pennsylvania.

Quilt size: 40½" x 49½"
Block size: 9" x 7½"

> I have always been impressed by Chinese art and architecture, so I was truly excited when I found the Chinese Screen pattern. Most coverlets consist of circles, squares, ovals, diamonds, or other standard geometric shapes, but the Chinese Screen pattern features a lattice design that is dramatically different. Pat, the quiltmaker, chose green for the background, which is somewhat reminiscent of rice paper, but you could experiment with other bold two-color combinations, such as red and black.

Materials

Yardage is based on 42"-wide fabric.

3⅜ yards of green print for blocks

2⅝ yards of teal print for blocks, border, and binding

2½ yards of fabric for backing

44" x 53" piece of batting

Cutting

From the teal print, cut:

16 strips, ¾" x 42"; cut *2 of the strips* into 4 strips, ¾" x 21" (1 will be extra)

1 strip, 6½" x 42"; cut into 2 strips, 6½" x 21" (1 will be extra)

17 strips, 1" x 42"

5 strips, 1¾" x 42"

1 strip, 1¼" x 42"

2 strips, 3" x 42"

1 strip, 2" x 42"

11 strips, 2½" x 42"

1 strip, 1½" x 42"

1 strip, 3½" x 42"; cut into 2 strips, 3½" x 21" (1 will be extra)

From the green print, cut:

11 strips, 1" x 42"; cut *2 of the strips* into 4 strips, 1" x 21" (1 will be extra)

5 strips, 1¼" x 42"

3 strips, 5½" x 42"

1 strip, 7" x 42"

2 strips, 7½" x 42"

4 strips, 5" x 42"

4 strips, ¾" x 42"

1 strip, 2" x 42"

1 strip, 2¼" x 42"

3 strips, 4" x 42"

1 strip, 1½" x 42"

1 strip, 3" x 42"

2 strips, 2½" x 42"

1 strip, 4¼" x 42"; cut into 2 strips, 4¼" x 21" (1 will be extra)

Assembling the Blocks

"Chinese Screen" requires 12 blocks (A) and 12 reverse blocks (B). Each block is made of 16 columns; the columns are simply sewn in reverse order to make the reverse blocks. We'll start by making the strip sets.

Making the Strip Sets

For this quilt, you'll make 16 strip sets, each in a different configuration. Sew the specified strips in order from left to right. Press the seam allowances in one direction.

Strip set number	Strip length	Strip width and color (T=Teal; G=Green)								
1	21"	¾" T	1" G	6½" T	1" G	¾" T	—	—	—	—
2	42"	1¼" G	1" T	5½" G	1" T	1¼" G	—	—	—	—
3	42"	1¾" T	5½" G	1¾" T	—	—	—	—	—	—
4*	42"	¾" T	7½" G	¾" T	—	—	—	—	—	—
5	42"	¾" T	7" G	1¼" T	—	—	—	—	—	—
6	42"	¾" T	5" G	3" T	¾" G	—	—	—	—	—
7	42"	¾" T	5" G	1" T	2" G	1" T	¾" G	—	—	—
8	42"	¾" T	5" G	1" T	1" G	1" T	1" G	1" T	¾" G	—
9	42"	¾" T	5" G	2" T	1" G	1" T	¾" G	—	—	—
10	42"	¾" T	5½" G	1" T	2¼" G	—	—	—	—	—
11	42"	¾" T	4" G	2½" T	1" G	1¾" T	—	—	—	—
12	42"	¾" T	4" G	1" T	1½" G	1" T	1" G	1" T	1¼" G	—
13	42"	¾" T	4" G	1" T	1" G	1½" T	1" G	1" T	1" G	¾" T
14	42"	1¾" T	3" G	1" T	2½" G	1" T	1¼" G	—	—	—
15	42"	1¼" G	1" T	2½" G	3" T	1" G	1¾" T	—	—	—
16	21"	¾" T	1" G	3½" T	4¼" G	—	—	—	—	—

*Make 2 of strip set 4.

Cutting the Columns

Cut the strip sets into segments of the specified widths to assemble the blocks. The segment width varies for each strip set, as indicated below. From each strip set, cut 24 segments, 12 for block A and 12 for block B.

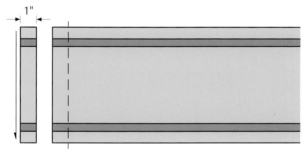

Strip set 2.
Cut 24 segments, 1" wide, for column 2.

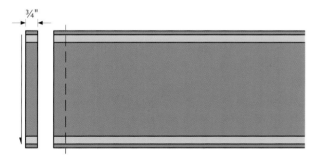

Strip set 1.
Cut 24 segments, ¾" wide, for column 1.

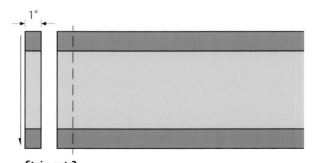

Strip set 3.
Cut 24 segments, 1" wide, for column 3.

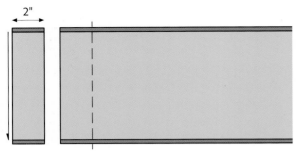

Strip set 4.
Cut 24 segments, 2" wide, for column 4.

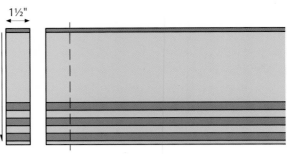

Strip set 8.
Cut 24 segments, 1½" wide, for column 8.

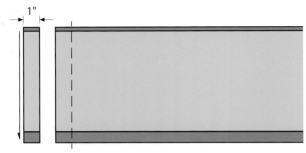

Strip set 5.
Cut 24 segments, 1" wide, for column 5.

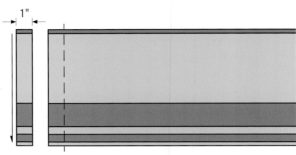

Strip set 9.
Cut 24 segments, 1" wide, for column 9.

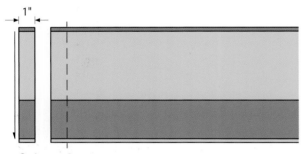

Strip set 6.
Cut 24 segments, 1" wide, for column 6.

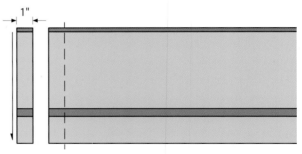

Strip set 10.
Cut 24 segments, 1" wide, for column 10.

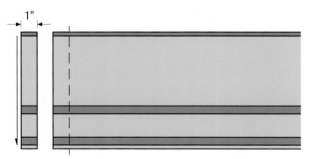

Strip set 7.
Cut 24 segments, 1" wide, for column 7.

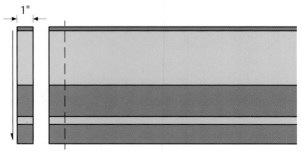

Strip set 11.
Cut 24 segments, 1" wide, for column 11.

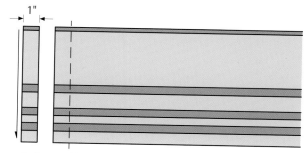

Strip set 12.

Cut 24 segments, 1" wide, for column 12.

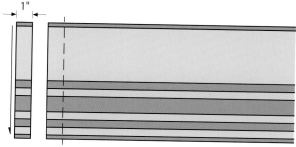

Strip set 13.

Cut 24 segments, 1" wide, for column 13.

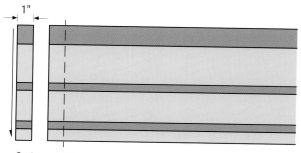

Strip set 14.

Cut 24 segments, 1" wide, for column 14.

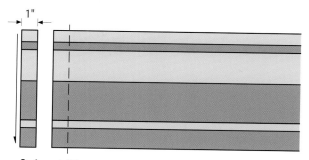

Strip set 15.

Cut 24 segments, 1" wide, for column 15.

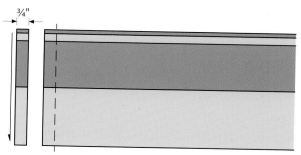

Strip set 16.

Cut 24 segments, ¾" wide, for column 16.

Completing the Blocks

1. Using one segment from each strip set as described, make 12 A blocks, sewing the columns in numerical order 1–16 from left to right. Press the seam allowances in one direction as shown.

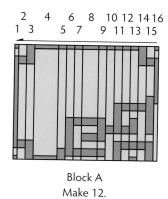

Block A
Make 12.

2. Using one segment from each strip set, make 12 B blocks by sewing the columns in reverse order 16–1 from left to right. Press the seam allowances in one direction as shown.

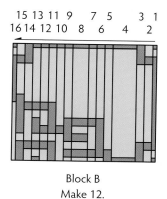

Block B
Make 12.

Assembling the Quilt

1. Arrange the blocks as shown in the quilt assembly diagram below. Note that some of the blocks are rotated 180° to form the quilt pattern.

2. Once your blocks are all arranged, sew them together in rows, pressing the seam allowances in opposite directions from row to row. Then sew the rows together and press the seam allowances in one direction. The quilt-top center should measure 36½" x 45½".

3. Join five of the teal 2½"-wide strips end to end. From the pieced strip, cut two 45½"-long strips and two 40½"-long strips. Sew the 45½"-long strips to opposite sides of the quilt top. Press the seam allowances toward the border. Sew the 40½"-long strips to the top and bottom of the quilt top. Press the seam allowances toward the border.

Finishing the Quilt

For details on any of the following steps, go to ShopMartingale.com/HowtoQuilt for free downloadable information.

1. Cut and piece the backing fabric and then layer the quilt top with batting and backing.

2. After basting the layers together, hand or machine quilt as desired. Trim the batting and backing so that the edges are even with the quilt top.

3. Using the remaining teal 2½"-wide strips, make and attach binding.

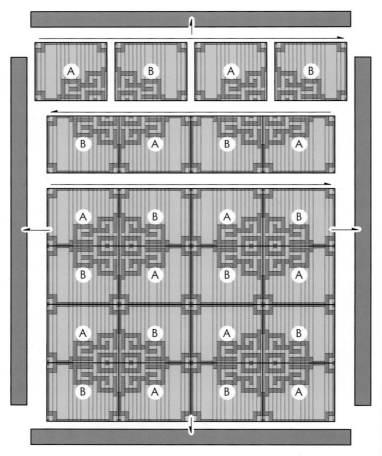

Quilt assembly

Charlotte's Garden

Pieced by Kelly Meanix, Downingtown, Pennsylvania, 2012. Quilted by Robin McMillen, Downingtown, Pennsylvania.

Quilt size: 42½" x 42½"
Block size: 9½" x 9½"

"The woven coverlet that inspired "Charlotte's Garden" is different in that the pattern forms stars and hearts. As a two-color quilt, for instance gold and black, it's truly striking with the star and heart-cloud configurations seeming to float in space. When I started playing with colors, the formal garden popped out and I immediately thought of our granddaughter Charlotte—serenely calm and beautiful—and so it became "Charlotte's Garden." This quilt features a block that I use in multiple quilts. If you rotate each block 180°, the hearts (or garden) are in the middle and the stars are in the corners (see page 91)."

Materials

Yardage is based on 42"-wide fabric.

2¼ yards of light-green print for blocks
1⅜ yards of plum print for blocks, border, and binding
1⅜ yards of pink print for blocks
½ yard of dark-green print for blocks
2¾ yards of fabric for backing
46" x 46" piece of batting

Cutting

From the plum print, cut:
6 strips, ¾" x 42"; cut *5 of the strips* into 10 strips, ¾" x 21"
1 strip, 3" x 42"; cut into 2 strips, 3" x 21"
1 strip, 1½" x 42"; cut into 2 strips, 1½" x 21"
6 strips, 1" x 42"; cut into 11 strips, 1" x 21" (1 will be extra)
1 strip, 1¾" x 42"; cut into 2 strips, 1¾" x 21"
1 strip, 1¼" x 42"; cut into 2 strips, 1¼" x 21"
10 strips, 2½" x 42"

From the dark-green print, cut:
2 strips, 1" x 42"; cut into 4 strips, 1" x 21" (1 will be extra)
1 strip, ¾" x 42"; cut into 2 strips, ¾" x 21" (1 will be extra)
2 strips, 3" x 42"; cut into 4 strips, 3" x 21"
1 strip, 1½" x 42"; cut into 2 strips, 1½" x 21"
1 strip, 2" x 42"; cut into 2 strips, 2" x 21"
1 strip, 2½" x 42"

From the light-green print, cut:
2 strips, 5" x 42"; cut into 4 strips, 5" x 21" (1 will be extra)
2 strips, 5½" x 42"; cut into 4 strips, 5½" x 21"
1 strip, 5¼" x 42"; cut into 2 strips, 5¼" x 21" (1 will be extra)
1 strip, 1¼" x 42"; cut into 2 strips, 1¼" x 21"
1 strip, 1¾" x 42"; cut into 2 strips, 1¾" x 21" (1 will be extra)
1 strip, 2¼" x 42"; cut into 2 strips, 2¼" x 21" (1 will be extra)
1 strip, 4½" x 42"; cut into 2 strips, 4½" x 21" (1 will be extra)
3 strips, ¾" x 42"; cut *2 of the strips* into 4 strips, ¾" x 21" (1 will be extra)
1 strip, 4¾" x 42"; cut into 2 strips, 4¾" x 21" (1 will be extra)
1 strip, 4¼" x 42"; cut into 2 strips, 4¼" x 21" (1 will be extra)
1 strip, 3¾" x 42"; cut into 2 strips, 3¾" x 21"
2 strips, 3½" x 42"; cut into 4 strips, 3½" x 21" (1 will be extra)
1 strip, 7¾" x 42"
1 strip, 6¾" x 42"

From the pink print, cut:
2 strips, 1" x 42"; cut into 4 strips, 1" x 21"
3 strips, ¾" x 42"; cut into 6 strips, ¾" x 21" (1 will be extra)
2 strips, 2" x 42"; cut into 4 strips, 2" x 21" (1 will be extra)
2 strips, 3" x 42"; cut into 4 strips, 3" x 21" (1 will be extra)
2 strips, 3½" x 42"; cut *1 of the strips* into 2 strips, 3½" x 21"
1 strip, 4" x 42"; cut into 2 strips, 4" x 21" (1 will be extra)
1 strip, 2½" x 42"; cut into 2 strips, 2½" x 21" (1 will be extra)
1 strip, 4½" x 42"; cut into 2 strips, 4½" x 21" (1 will be extra)
2 strips, 5" x 42"; cut into 4 strips, 5" x 21" (1 will be extra)
1 strip, 1½" x 42"; cut into 2 strips, 1½" x 21" (1 will be extra)

Assembling the Blocks

"Charlotte's Garden" requires eight blocks (A) and eight reverse blocks (B). Each block is made of 18 columns; the columns are simply sewn in reverse order to make the reverse blocks. We'll start by making the strip sets.

Making the Strip Sets

For this quilt, you'll make 18 strip sets, each in a different configuration. Sew the specified strips in order from left to right. Press the seam allowances in one direction.

Strip set number	Strip length	Strip width and color (LG=Light green; P=Plum; PK=Pink; G=Dark green)						
1	21"	¾" P	1" G	3" P	5" LG	1" PK	1½" P	¾" PK
2	21"	¾" G	1" P	3" G	5½" LG	1¾" P	—	—
3	21"	¾" P	1" G	1" P	3" G	5½" LG	1¼" P	—
4	21"	¾" P	1½" G	1" P	3" G	5½" LG	¾" PK	—
5	21"	¾" P	2" G	1" P	3" G	5¼" LG	—	—
6	42"	¾" P	2½" G	7¾" LG	—	—	—	—
7	21"	1¼" LG	2" G	5½" LG	2" PK	1¼" LG	—	—
8	21"	1¾" LG	1½" G	5" LG	3" PK	¾" LG	—	—
9	21"	2¼" LG	1" G	4½" LG	3½" PK	¾" LG	—	—
10	42"	6¾" LG	3½" PK	¾" LG	—	—	—	—
11	21"	4¾" LG	2" PK	1" P	3½" PK	¾" LG	—	—
12	21"	4¼" LG	3" PK	1" P	3" PK	¾" P	—	—
13	21"	3¾" LG	4" PK	1" P	2½" PK	¾" P	—	—
14	21"	3¾" LG	4½" PK	1" P	2" PK	¾" P	—	—
15	21"	¾" PK	3½" LG	5" PK	1" P	1½" PK	¾" P	—
16	21"	1¼" P	3½" LG	5" PK	1" P	1" PK	¾" P	—
17	21"	1¾" P	3½" LG	5" PK	1" P	¾"PK	—	—
18	21"	¾" PK	1½" P	1" PK	5" LG	3" P	1" PK	¾" P

Cutting the Columns

Cut the strip sets into segments of the specified widths to assemble the blocks. The segment width varies for each strip set, as indicated below. From each strip set, cut 16 segments, 8 for block A and 8 for block B.

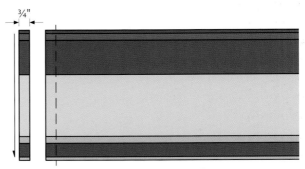

¾"

Strip set 1.
Cut 16 segments, ¾" wide, for column 1.

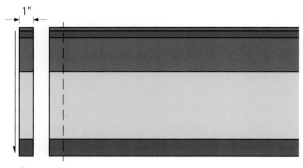

Strip set 2.
Cut 16 segments, 1" wide, for column 2.

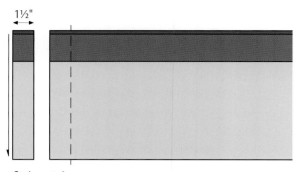

Strip set 6.
Cut 16 segments, 1½" wide, for column 6.

Strip set 3.
Cut 16 segments, 1" wide, for column 3.

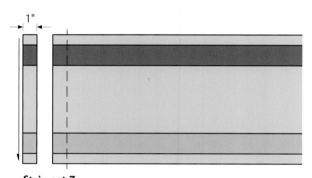

Strip set 7.
Cut 16 segments, 1" wide, for column 7.

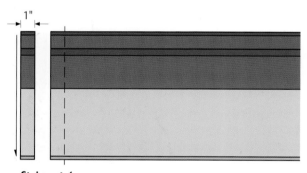

Strip set 4.
Cut 16 segments, 1" wide, for column 4.

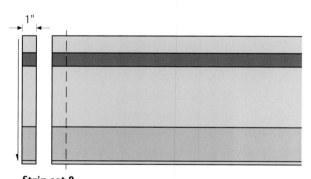

Strip set 8.
Cut 16 segments, 1" wide, for column 8.

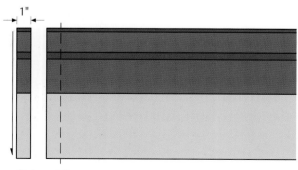

Strip set 5.
Cut 16 segments, 1" wide, for column 5.

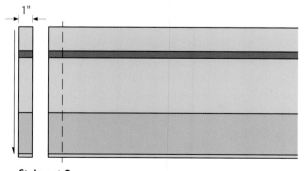

Strip set 9.
Cut 16 segments, 1" wide, for column 9.

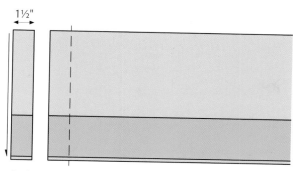

Strip set 10.
Cut 16 segments, 1½" wide, for column 10.

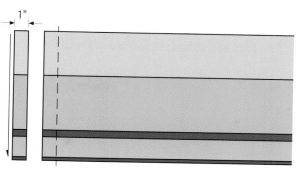

Strip set 14.
Cut 16 segments, 1" wide, for column 14.

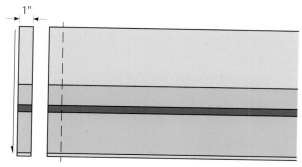

Strip set 11.
Cut 16 segments, 1" wide, for column 11.

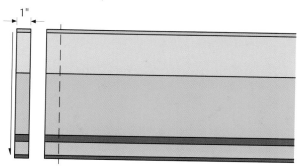

Strip set 15.
Cut 16 segments, 1" wide, for column 15.

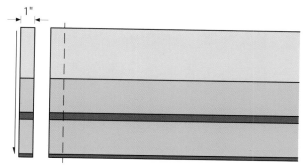

Strip set 12.
Cut 16 segments, 1" wide, for column 12.

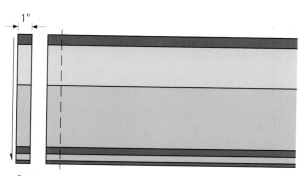

Strip set 16.
Cut 16 segments, 1" wide, for column 16.

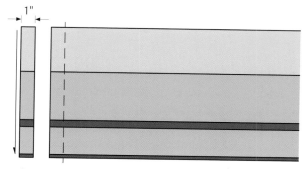

Strip set 13.
Cut 16 segments, 1" wide, for column 13.

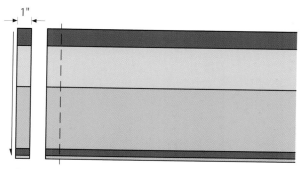

Strip set 17.
Cut 16 segments, 1" wide, for column 17.

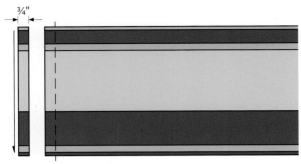

Strip set 18.
Cut 16 segments, ¾" wide, for column 18.

Completing the Blocks

1. Using one segment from each strip set as described, make eight A blocks, sewing the columns in numerical order 1–18 from left to right. Press the seam allowances in one direction as shown.

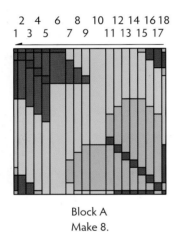

Block A
Make 8.

2. Using one segment from each strip set, make eight B blocks by sewing the columns in reverse order 18–1 from left to right. Press the seam allowances in one direction as shown.

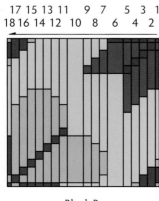

Block B
Make 8.

Assembling the Quilt

1. Arrange the blocks as shown in the quilt assembly diagram below. Note that some of the blocks are rotated 180° to form the quilt pattern.

2. Once your blocks are all arranged, sew them together in rows, pressing the seam allowances in opposite directions from row to row. Then sew the rows together and press the seam allowances in one direction. The quilt-top center should measure 38½" square.

3. Join five of the plum 2½"-wide strips end to end. From the pieced strip, cut two 38½"-long strips and two 42½"-long strips. Sew the 38½"-long strips to opposite sides of the quilt top. Press the seam allowances toward the border. Sew the 42½"-long strips to the top and bottom of the quilt top. Press the seam allowances toward the border.

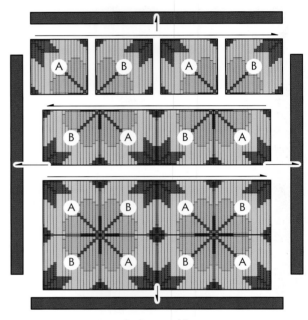

Quilt assembly

Finishing the Quilt

For details on any of the following steps, go to ShopMartingale.com/HowtoQuilt for free downloadable information.

1. Cut and piece the backing fabric and then layer the quilt top with batting and backing.

2. After basting the layers together, hand or machine quilt as desired. Trim the batting and backing so that the edges are even with the quilt top.

3. Using the remaining plum 2½"-wide strips, make and attach binding.

Ezekiel's Wheel

Pieced by Sara Borr, Downingtown, Pennsylvania, 2012. Quilted by Carol Lee Heisler, Lorac Designs, East Norriton, Pennsylvania.

Quilt size: 36½" x 36½"
Block size: 8" x 8"

"My quest for converting woven coverlets into quilts began with this quilt. When I first saw the coverlet, I knew that it would make an incredible quilt. The circles, along with the curved diamond center and the overlaying on-point square, convey a graphic clarity that is almost perfect. In addition, the block is one of the easiest to construct and lends itself easily to multiple variations (see page 91)."

Materials

Yardage is based on 42"-wide fabric.

1⅞ yards of yellow print for blocks
1¼ yards of blue print for blocks and border
⅜ yard of blue stripe for binding
1¼ yards of fabric for backing
40" x 40" piece of batting

Cutting

From the blue print, cut:
14 strips, 1" x 42"
2 strips, 1¼" x 42"
6 strips, 1¾" x 42"
2 strips, 2½" x 32½"
2 strips, 2½" x 36½"

From the yellow print, cut:
4 strips, 1" x 42"
2 strips, 1½" x 42"
6 strips, 2" x 42"
2 strips, 4" x 42"
4 strips, 2¼" x 42"
2 strips, 1¼" x 42"
4 strips, 3½" x 42"
2 strips, 4¼" x 42"

From the blue stripe, cut:
4 strips, 2½" x 42"

Assembling the Blocks

"Ezekiel's Wheel" requires eight blocks (A) and eight reverse blocks (B). Each block is made of 11 columns; the columns are simply sewn in reverse order to make the reverse blocks. There are multiple repeats among the columns so you only need four strip sets. We'll start by making the strip sets.

Making the Strip Sets

For this quilt, you'll use four different strip-set configurations as listed in the table below. Sew the specified strips in order from left to right. Press the seam allowances in one direction. Make two of *each* strip set.

Strip set number	Strip length	Strip width and color (B=Blue; Y=Yellow)						
1	42"	1" B	2" Y	1" B	1¼" Y	1" B	4¼" Y	1" B
2	42"	1" Y	1" B	2" Y	1¼" B	3½" Y	1¾" B	1" Y
3	42"	1½" Y	1" B	4" Y	1¾" B	2¼" Y	—	—
4	42"	2" Y	1" B	2¼" Y	1¾" B	3½" Y	—	—

Cutting the Columns

Cut the strip sets into segments of the specified widths and quantities to assemble blocks A and B. The segment width varies for each strip set, as indicated below.

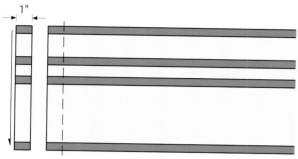

Strip set 1. Make 2.
Cut 16 segments, 1" wide, for column 1
(8 for block A and 8 for block B).
Cut 16 segments, 1" wide, for column 5
(8 for block A and 8 for block B).
Cut 16 segments, 1" wide, for column 7
(8 for block A and 8 for block B).
Cut 16 segments, 1" wide, for column 11
(8 for block A and 8 for block B).

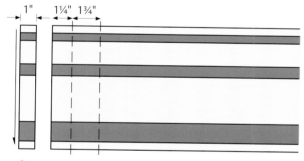

Strip set 2. Make 2.
Cut 16 segments, 1" wide, for column 2
(8 for block A and 8 for block B).
Cut 16 segments, 1¼" wide, for column 6
(8 for block A and 8 for block B).
Cut 16 segments, 1¾" wide, for column 10
(8 for block A and 8 for block B).

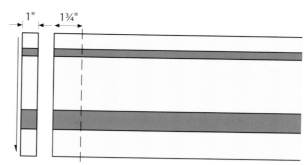

Strip set 3. Make 2.
Cut 16 segments, 1" wide, for column 3
(8 for block A and 8 for block B).
Cut 16 segments, 1¾" wide, for column 9
(8 for block A and 8 for block B).

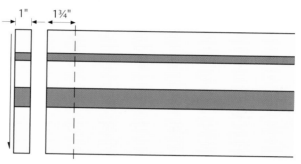

Strip set 4. Make 2.
Cut 16 segments, 1" wide, for column 4
(8 for block A and 8 for block B).
Cut 16 segments, 1¾" wide, for column 8
(8 for block A and 8 for block B).

Completing the Blocks

1. Using one segment from each strip set as described, make eight A blocks, sewing the columns in numerical order 1–11 from left to right. Press the seam allowances in one direction as shown.

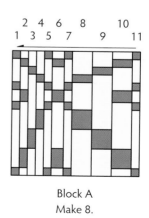

Block A
Make 8.

2. Using one segment from each strip set, make eight B blocks by sewing the columns in reverse order 11–1 from left to right. Press the seam allowances in one direction as shown.

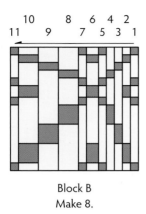

Block B
Make 8.

Assembling the Quilt

1. Arrange the blocks as shown in the quilt assembly diagram below. Note that some of the blocks are rotated 180° to form the quilt pattern.

2. Once your blocks are all arranged, sew them together in rows, pressing the seam allowances in opposite directions from row to row. Then sew the rows together and press the seam allowances in one direction. The quilt-top center should measure 32½" square.

3. Sew the blue 32½"-long strips to opposite sides of the quilt top. Press the seam allowances toward the border. Sew the blue 36½"-long strips to the top and bottom of the quilt top. Press the seam allowances toward the border.

Finishing the Quilt

For details on any of the following steps, go to ShopMartingale.com/HowtoQuilt for free downloadable information.

1. Cut and piece the backing fabric and then layer the quilt top with batting and backing.

2. After basting the layers together, hand or machine quilt as desired. Trim the batting and backing so that the edges are even with the quilt top.

3. Using the blue-striped 2½"-wide strips, make and attach binding.

Quilt assembly

Miranda's Puzzle

Pieced by Jean Fox, West Chester, Pennsylvania, 2012. Quilted by Kathleen DeCarli, Downingtown, Pennsylvania.

Quilt size: 34½" x 34½"
Block size: 7½" x 7½"

"I originally used black and gold for this design, with a complex and graphically stunning result. For this book, however, I decided to make a multicolored version, and when Kathleen added the colors, the puzzle effect emerged. The effect reminded me of my granddaughter Miranda, who routinely puts together 1,000-piece puzzles while simultaneously doing her homework and working on a robot. So, the quilt became "Miranda's Puzzle." The block can be used to create multiple quilt patterns, and if you turn each block 180°, you get the arrow configuration in the middle and the stars in the corners (see page 92)."

Materials

Yardage is based on 42"-wide fabric.
1½ yards of beige print for blocks
1⅜ yards of green print for blocks, border, and binding
⅝ yard of yellow print for blocks
½ yard of pink print for blocks
¼ yard of blue print for blocks
1¼ yards of fabric for backing
38" x 38" piece of batting

Cutting

From the yellow print, cut:
3 strips, ¾" x 42"; cut into 6 strips, ¾" x 21"
1 strip, 2" x 42"; cut into 2 strips, 2" x 21"
4 strips, 1" x 42"; cut into 8 strips, 1" x 21"
2 strips, 1½" x 42"; cut into 4 strips, 1½" x 21" (1 will be extra)
1 strip, 1¼" x 42"; cut into 2 strips, 1¼" x 21" (1 will be extra)
1 strip, 3" x 42"; cut into 2 strips, 3" x 21" (1 will be extra)

From the beige print, cut:
6 strips, 1½" x 42"; cut into 12 strips, 1½" x 21"
5 strips, 2" x 42"; cut into 10 strips, 2" x 21"
4 strips, ¾" x 42"; cut into 8 strips, ¾" x 21" (1 will be extra)
3 strips, 2½" x 42"; cut into 6 strips, 2½" x 21"
2 strips, 1¼" x 42"; cut into 4 strips, 1¼" x 21"
4 strips, 1" x 42"; cut into 8 strips, 1" x 21"
1 strip, 3½" x 42"; cut into 2 strips, 3½" x 21" (1 will be extra)
1 strip, 1¾" x 42"; cut into 2 strips, 1¾" x 21"
1 strip, 3" x 42"; cut into 2 strips, 3" x 21" (1 will be extra)
1 strip, 4" x 42"; cut into 2 strips, 4" x 21" (1 will be extra)

From the pink print, cut:
1 strip, 2½" x 42"; cut into 2 strips, 2½" x 21"
2 strips, 2" x 42"; cut into 4 strips, 2" x 21"
1 strip, 1¾" x 42"; cut into 2 strips, 1¾" x 21"
1 strip, 1¼" x 42"; cut into 2 strips, 1¼" x 21"
2 strips, ¾" x 42"; cut into 4 strips, ¾" x 21"

From the blue print, cut:
1 strip, 1½" x 42"; cut into 2 strips, 1½" x 21"
1 strip, 1¼" x 42"; cut into 2 strips, 1¼" x 21"
1 strip, ¾" x 42"; cut into 2 strips, ¾" x 21"

From the green print, cut:
4 strips, 1" x 42"; cut into 8 strips, 1" x 21" (1 will be extra)
5 strips, 1½" x 42"; cut into 10 strips, 1½" x 21" (1 will be extra)
2 strips, 2½" x 42"; cut into 4 strips, 2½" x 21"
1 strip, 2" x 42"; cut into 2 strips, 2" x 21" (1 will be extra)
1 strip, 3" x 42"; cut into 2 strips, 3" x 21"
2 strips, 2½" x 30½"
2 strips, 2½" x 34½"
4 strips, 2½" x 42"

Assembling the Blocks

"Miranda's Puzzle" requires eight blocks (A) and eight reverse blocks (B). Each block is made of 16 columns; the columns are simply sewn in reverse order to make the reverse blocks. We'll start by making the strip sets.

Making the Strip Sets

For this quilt, you'll make 16 strip sets, each in a different configuration. Sew the specified strips in order from left to right. Press the seam allowances in one direction.

Strip set number	Strip length	Strip width and color (G=Green; B=Beige; Y=Yellow; P=Pink; BL=Blue)									
1	21"	¾" Y	1½" B	2" Y	2" B	2½" P	1½" BL	¾" Y	—	—	—
2	21"	¾" B	1" Y	2" B	1½" Y	2½" B	2" P	1¼" BL	—	—	—
3	21"	1¼" B	1" Y	2" B	1½" Y	2½" B	2" P	¾" BL	—	—	—
4	21"	¾" Y	1½" B	1" Y	1" B	3" Y	2" B	1¾" P	—	—	—
5	21"	¾" Y	2" B	1" Y	3½" B	1" G	1½" B	1¼" P	—	—	—
6	21"	1¼" Y	1" B	1" Y	1" B	1" G	2½" B	1½" G	2" B	¾" P	—
7	21"	¾" B	2" Y	1½" B	1½" G	1" B	1" G	1" B	1½" G	1½" B	¾" P
8	21"	1¼" B	1½" Y	1½" B	2½" G	1" B	1½" G	1¾" B	—	—	—
9	21"	1¾" B	1" Y	2" B	2" G	1½" B	1½" G	1¼" B	—	—	—
10	21"	¾" P	1½" B	1" Y	1½" B	3" G	1" B	1½" G	1¼" B	—	—
11	21"	¾" P	2½" B	1" G	2" B	1½" G	1½" B	1½" G	¾" B	—	—
12	21"	1¼" P	1½" B	2½" G	2" B	1" G	1" B	1½" G	¾" B	—	—
13	21"	1¾" P	2" B	2½" G	2½" B	1" G	¾"B	—	—	—	—
14	21"	¾" BL	2" P	2½" B	2½" G	1½"B	1" G	¾" B	—	—	—
15	21"	1¼" BL	2" P	3" B	3" G	¾" Y	—	—	—	—	—
16	21"	¾" Y	1½" BL	2½" P	4" B	1" Y	¾" B	—	—	—	—

Cutting the Columns

Cut the strip sets into segments of the specified widths to assemble the blocks. The segment width varies for each strip set, as indicated below. From each strip set, cut 16 segments, 8 for block A and 8 for block B.

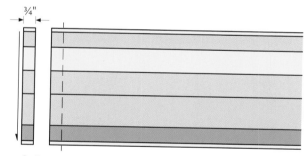

Strip set 1.
Cut 16 segments, ¾" wide, for column 1.

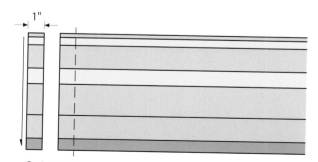

Strip set 2.
Cut 16 segments, 1" wide, for column 2.

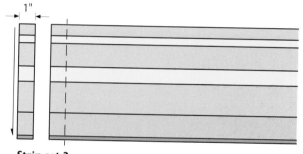

Strip set 3.
Cut 16 segments, 1" wide, for column 3.

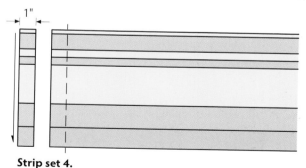

Strip set 4.
Cut 16 segments, 1" wide, for column 4.

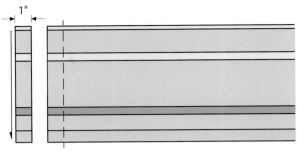

Strip set 5.
Cut 16 segments, 1" wide, for column 5.

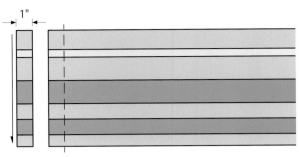

Strip set 9.
Cut 16 segments, 1" wide, for column 9.

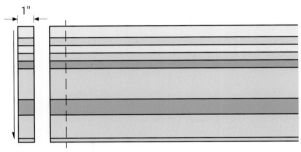

Strip set 6.
Cut 16 segments, 1" wide, for column 6.

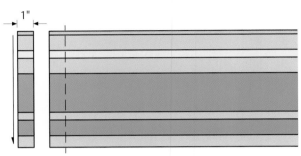

Strip set 10.
Cut 16 segments, 1" wide, for column 10.

Strip set 7.
Cut 16 segments, 1" wide, for column 7.

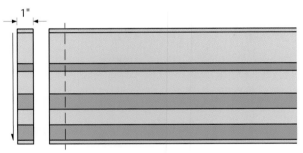

Strip set 11.
Cut 16 segments, 1" wide, for column 11.

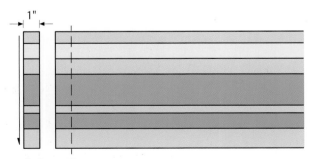

Strip set 8.
Cut 16 segments, 1" wide, for column 8.

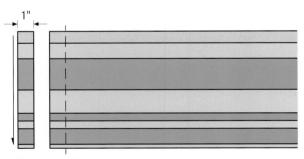

Strip set 12.
Cut 16 segments, 1" wide, for column 12.

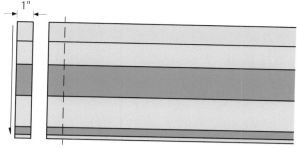

1"

Strip set 13.
Cut 16 segments, 1" wide, for column 13.

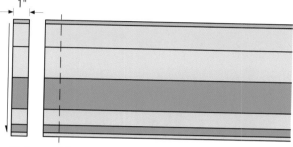

1"

Strip set 14.
Cut 16 segments, 1" wide, for column 14.

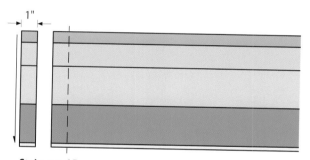

1"

Strip set 15.
Cut 16 segments, 1" wide, for column 15.

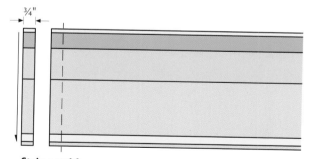

¾"

Strip set 16.
Cut 16 segments, ¾" wide, for column 16.

Completing the Blocks

1. Using one segment from each strip set as described, make eight A blocks, sewing the columns in numerical order 1–16 from left to right. Press the seam allowances in one direction as shown.

2 4 6 8 10 12 14 16
1 3 5 7 9 11 13 15

Block A
Make 8.

2. Using one segment from each strip set, make eight B blocks by sewing the columns in reverse order 16–1 from left to right. Press the seam allowances in one direction as shown.

15 13 11 9 7 5 3 1
16 14 12 10 8 6 4 2

Block B
Make 8.

Assembling the Quilt

1. Arrange the blocks as shown in the quilt assembly diagram on page 52. Note that some of the blocks are rotated 180° to form the quilt pattern.

2. Once your blocks are all arranged, sew them together in rows, pressing the seam allowances in opposite directions from row to row. Then sew the rows together and press the seam allowances in one direction. The quilt-top center should measure 30½" square.

3. Sew the green 30½"-long strips to opposite sides of the quilt top. Press the seam allowances toward the border. Sew the green 34½"-long strips to the top and bottom of the quilt top. Press the seam allowances toward the border.

Finishing the Quilt

For details on any of the following steps, go to ShopMartingale.com/HowtoQuilt for free downloadable information.

1. Cut and piece the backing fabric and then layer the quilt top with batting and backing.

2. After basting the layers together, hand or machine quilt as desired. Trim the batting and backing so that the edges are even with the quilt top.

3. Using the green 2½" x 42" strips, make and attach binding.

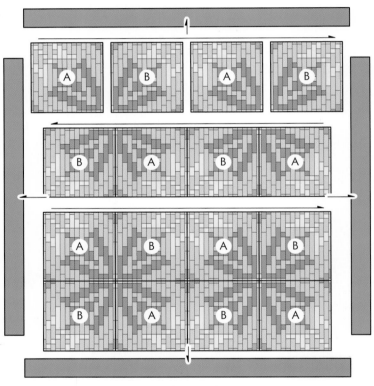

Quilt assembly

Monarch

Pieced and quilted by Cindy Vognetz, Phoenixville, Pennsylvania, 2012. Quilted by Barb Persing, Frederick, Pennsylvania.

Quilt size: 41½" x 47½"
Block size: 9" x 10½"

> As I began my journey through the world of woven coverlets, I had no idea as to the geometric complexity that I would find. I was well into my journey before I found the coverlet that inspired "Monarch," which contained none of the standard geometric shapes. It was a black-and-white drawing and looked sort of like a stylized flower. Kathleen played with the colors in the quilt design and the vibrant "Monarch" you see here emerged.

Materials

Yardage is based on 42"-wide fabric.

1⅔ yards of black print for blocks, accent border, and binding

1⅜ yards of light-green print for blocks

1¼ yards of orange print for blocks

1 yard of plum print for blocks and outer border

2 yards of fabric for backing

44" x 50" piece of batting

Cutting

From the plum print, cut:

4 strips, 1" x 42"; cut *1 of the strips* into 2 strips, 1" x 21" (1 will be extra)

5 strips, ¾" x 42"; cut *2 of the strips* into 4 strips, ¾" x 21"

3 strips, 1½" x 42"; cut into 6 strips, 1½" x 21"

1 strip, 1¼" x 42"

5 strips, 3" x 42"

From the light-green print, cut:

3 strips, 2" x 42"; cut *1 of the strips* into 2 strips, 2" x 21" (1 will be extra)

1 strip, 8½" x 42"

4 strips, 1½" x 42"; cut *3 of the strips* into 6 strips, 1½" x 21" (1 will be extra)

1 strips, 3½" x 42"; cut into 2 strips, 3½" x 21"

2 strips, 1¾" x 42"

1 strip, 4" x 42"

4 strips, 1¼" x 42"; cut *2 of the strips* into 4 strips, 1¼" x 21" (1 will be extra)

1 strip, 2½" x 42"; cut into 2 strips, 2½" x 21"

1 strip, 3" x 42"

3 strips, ¾" x 42"; cut into 6 strips, ¾" x 21" (1 will be extra)

From the black print, cut:

1 strip, 4½" x 42"; cut into 2 strips, 4½" x 21"

2 strips, 2" x 42"; cut *1 of the strips* into 2 strips, 2" x 21" (1 will be extra)

8 strips, 1" x 42"; cut *1 of the strips* into 2 strips, 1" x 21" (1 will be extra)

1 strip, 3½" x 42"; cut into 2 strips, 3½" x 21"

2 strips, 1½" x 42"; cut into 4 strips, 1½" x 21"

1 strip, 2¼" x 42"

1 strip, 3¾" x 42"; cut into 2 strips, 3¾" x 21"

8 strips, 2½" x 42"

1 strip, 1¼" x 42"

1 strip, ¾" x 42"

From the orange print, cut:

2 strips, 2½" x 42"; cut *1 of the strips* into 2 strips, 2½" x 21"

2 strips, 4¼" x 42"; cut *1 of the strips* into 2 strips, 4¼" x 21"

1 strip, 6½" x 42"; cut into 2 strips, 6½" x 21" (1 will be extra)

1 strip, 3½" x 42"

2 strips, 1½" x 42"; cut *1 of the strips* into 2 strips, 1½" x 21" (1 will be extra)

1 strip, 5" x 42"

1 strip, 2" x 42"

1 strip, ¾" x 42"; cut into 2 strips, ¾" x 21" (1 will be extra)

1 strip, 1¼" x 42"; cut into 2 strips, 1¼" x 21" (1 will be extra)

Assembling the Blocks

"Monarch" requires eight blocks (A) and eight reverse blocks (B). Each block is made of 13 columns; the columns are simply sewn in reverse order to make the reverse blocks. We'll start by making the strip sets.

Making the Strip Sets

For this quilt, you'll make 12 strip sets, each in a different configuration. Sew the specified strips in order from left to right. Press the seam allowances in one direction.

Strip set number	Strip length	Strip width and color (B=Black; G=Light green; P=Plum; O=Orange)						
1	42"	¾" P	2" G	1" P	8½" G	¾" P	—	—
2	21"	¾" P	1½" G	1½" P	3½" G	4½" B	1½" G	¾" P
3	42"	1¾" G	1" P	4" G	2" B	2½" O	1" B	1¾" G
4	21"	1¼" G	1½" P	2½" G	3½" B	2½" O	1½" B	1¼" G
5	42"	1¼" G	1" P	3" G	2¼" B	4¼" O	1" B	1¼" G
6	21"	¾" G	1½" P	1½" G	3¾" B	4¼" O	1½" B	¾" G
7	21"	¾" G	1" P	2" G	2" B	6½" O	1" B	¾" G
8	42"	1¼" P	1½" G	2½" B	3½" O	2½" B	1½" O	1¼" B
9	42"	¾" P	2" G	1" B	5" O	2½" B	2" O	¾" B
10	21"	¾" G	1½" P	1½" G	3¾" B	4¼" O	1½" B	¾" O
11	21"	1¼" G	1½" P	2½" G	3½" B	2½" O	1½" B	1¼" O
12	21"	¾" P	1½" G	1½" P	3½" G	4½" B	1½" O	¾" P

Cutting the Columns

Cut the strip sets into segments of the specified widths to assemble the blocks. The segment width varies for each strip set, as indicated below. From each strip set (except strip set 8), cut 16 segments, 8 for block A and 8 for block B. From strip set 8, cut 32 segments, 16 for block A and 16 for block B.

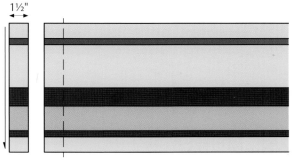

Strip set 3.
Cut 16 segments, 1½" wide, for column 3.

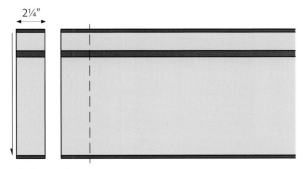

Strip set 1.
Cut 16 segments, 2¼" wide, for column 1.

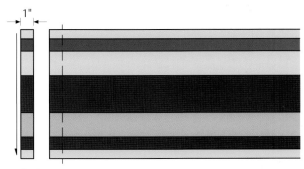

Strip set 4.
Cut 16 segments, 1" wide, for column 4.

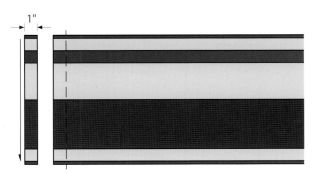

Strip set 2.
Cut 16 segments, 1" wide, for column 2.

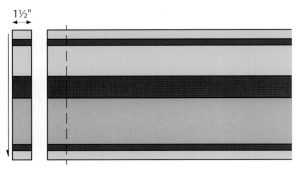

Strip set 5.
Cut 16 segments, 1½" wide, for column 5.

Strip set 6.
Cut 16 segments, 1" wide, for column 6.

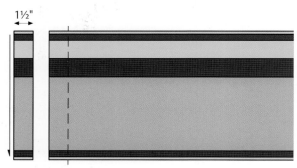

Strip set 7.
Cut 16 segments, 1½" wide, for column 7.

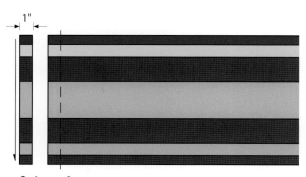

Strip set 8.
Cut 32 segments, 1" wide, for columns 8 and 10.

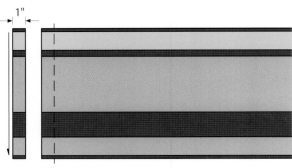

Strip set 9.
Cut 16 segments, 1" wide, for column 9.

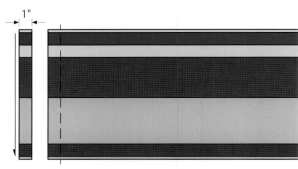

Strip set 10.
Cut 16 segments, 1" wide, for column 11.

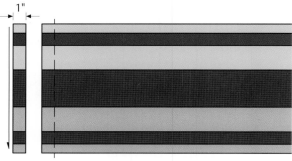

Strip set 11.
Cut 16 segments, 1" wide, for column 12.

Strip set 12.
Cut 16 segments, ¾" wide, for column 13.

Completing the Blocks

1. Using one segment from each strip set as described, make eight A blocks, sewing the columns in numerical order 1–13 from left to right. Press the seam allowances in one direction as shown.

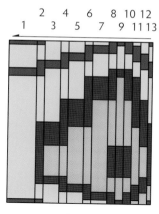

Block A
Make 8.

2. Using one segment from each strip set, make eight B blocks by sewing the columns in reverse order 13–1 from left to right. Press the seam allowances in one direction as shown.

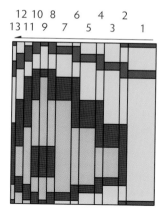

Block B
Make 8.

Assembling the Quilt

1. Arrange the blocks as shown in the quilt assembly diagram on page 58. Note that some of the blocks are rotated 180° to form the quilt pattern.

2. Once your blocks are all arranged, sew them together in rows, pressing the seam allowances in opposite directions from row to row. Then sew the rows together and press the seam allowances in one direction. The quilt-top center should measure 36½" x 42½".

3. To make the border accent, join the four remaining black 1"-wide strips end to end to make one continuous strip. Fold the long strip in half lengthwise, wrong sides together, and press. From the strip, cut two 36½"-long strips and two 42½"-long strips.

4. Position the raw edges of the accent strips even with the quilt-top edges. Baste the 42½"-long strips to the side edges of the quilt top using a scant ¼" seam allowance. Baste the 36½"-long strips to the top and bottom edges of the quilt top, overlapping the strips in the corners.

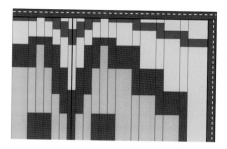

5. Join the plum 3"-wide strips end to end. From the pieced strip, cut two 42½"-long strips and two 41½"-long strips. Sew the 42½"-long strips to opposite sides of the quilt top. Press the seam allowances toward the border. Sew the 41½"-long strips to the top and bottom of the quilt top. Press the seam allowances toward the border.

Finishing the Quilt

For details on any of the following steps, go to ShopMartingale.com/HowtoQuilt for free downloadable information.

1. Cut and piece the backing fabric and then layer the quilt top with batting and backing.

2. After basting the layers together, hand or machine quilt as desired. Trim the batting and backing so that the edges are even with the quilt top.

3. Using the remaining black 2½"-wide strips, make and attach binding.

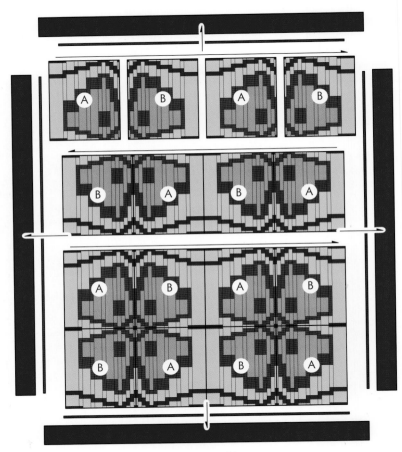

Quilt assembly

Red Lion

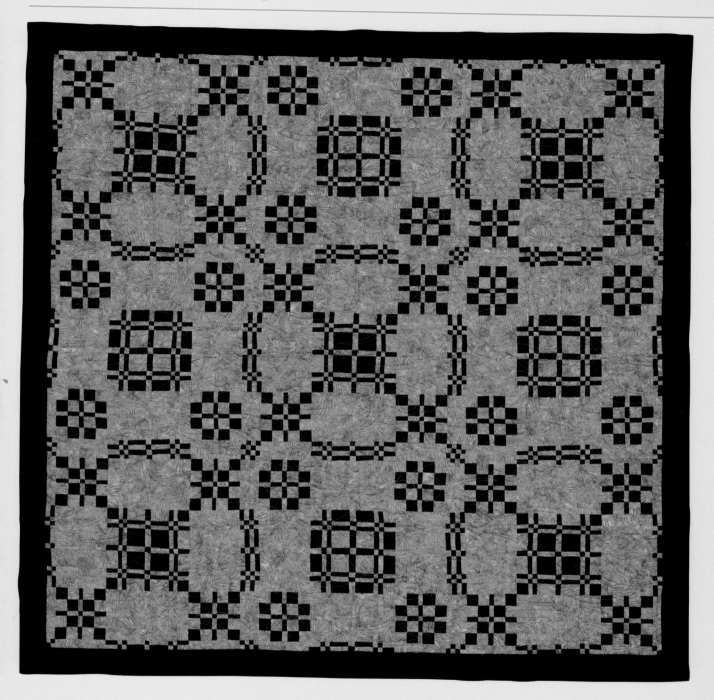

Pieced by Myrna Paluba, Wayne, Pennsylvania, 2012. Quilted by Carol Lee Heisler,
Lorac Designs, East Norriton, Pennsylvania.

Quilt size: 70½" x 70½"
Block size: 11" x 11"

> nce I started my quest for weaving patterns, I found them everywhere.
> At a gift shop in a quilt museum in Lancaster, Pennsylvania, I found a
> beautiful coverlet. When I asked to copy the pattern, the salesperson told me
> that it was a coverlet from the Family Heirloom Weaving Company in Red
> Lion, Pennsylvania. Kathleen and I made the trek to this amazing place. The
> owner, David Kline, has been in business for over 50 years and is still going
> strong. He gave us a tour of the entire factory, showing us how each of the
> machines worked. One loom had 2,200 Jacquard cards, with the warp threads
> forming a gigantic spiderweb. In a small gift shop I found a black and red
> coverlet that became "Red Lion." Myrna Paluba, the quiltmaker, chose to make
> it in green and black prints, but I left the name alone to honor the quilt's origin.

Materials

Yardage is based on 42"-wide fabric.
5½ yards of green print for blocks
3½ yards of black print for blocks, border, and binding
4⅜ yards of fabric for backing
74" x 74" piece of batting

Cutting

From the black print, cut:
24 strips, 1" x 42"
20 strips, 2½" x 42"
21 strips, 1¾" x 42"
5 strips, ¾" x 42"

From the green print, cut:
5 strips, 7¾" x 42"
19 strips, 1" x 42"
5 strips, ¾" x 42"
5 strips, 6" x 42"
5 strips, 2½" x 42"
4 strips, 1½" x 42"
8 strips, 1¾" x 42"
4 strips, 5" x 42"
4 strips, 2¾" x 42"
4 strips, 6¼" x 42"

Assembling the Blocks

"Red Lion" requires 10 blocks (A) and 10 reverse blocks (B). You also need 8 blocks (C) and 8 reverse blocks (D). Each block is made of 12 columns; the columns are simply sewn in reverse order to make the reverse blocks. This is one of the friendliest of the weaving-design quilts. Since there are multiple repeats among the columns, you only need four strip sets to make the entire quilt. We'll start by making the strip sets.

Basic Circle Block

Block A is just the basic circle block, common to many of the woven coverlets. Other quilts with a circle block include "Sunny South" (page 16), "Wedding Ring" (page 20), "Ludwig's Corner" (page 26), "Ezekiel's Wheel" (page 43), and "Thirteen States" (page 68). You could make a quilt using just the A and B blocks or just the C and D blocks. Design ideas can be found in "Variations on a Theme" starting on page 90.

Making the Strip Sets

For this quilt, you'll use four different strip-set configurations. Sew the specified strips in order from left to right. Press the seam allowances in one direction. Make five *each* of strip sets 1 and 2. Make four *each* of strip sets 3 and 4.

Strip set number	Strip length	Strip width and color (G=Green; B=Black)							
1	42"	1" B	7¾" G	1" B	1" G	2½" B	¾" G	—	—
2	42"	1" G	1" B	6" G	1¾" B	1" G	1" B	2½" G	¾" B
3	42"	1½" G	1¾" B	1¾" G	1" B	1¾" G	1¾" B	5" G	—
4	42"	2¾" G	1¾" B	1" G	1¾" B	6¼" G	—	—	—

Cutting the Columns

Cut the strip sets into segments of the specified widths and quantities to assemble blocks A, B, C, and D. The segment width varies for each strip set, as indicated in each illustration.

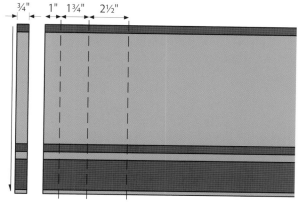

Strip set 1. Make 5.

Cut 20 segments, 1" wide, for column 1
(10 for block A and 10 for block B).

Cut 20 segments, 1" wide, for column 9
(10 for block A and 10 for block B).

Cut 20 segments, 2½" wide, for column 11
(10 for block A and 10 for block B).

Cut 16 segments, 1" wide, for column 2
(8 for block C and 8 for block D).

Cut 16 segments, 1¾" wide, for column 8
(8 for block C and 8 for block D).

Cut 16 segments, 1" wide, for column 10
(8 for block C and 8 for block D).

Cut 16 segments, ¾" wide, for column 12
(8 for block C and 8 for block D).

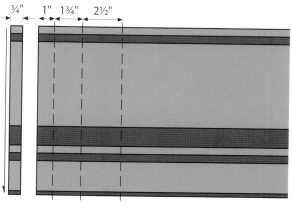

Strip set 2. Make 5.

Cut 20 segments, 1" wide, for column 2
(10 for block A and 10 for block B).

Cut 20 segments, 1¾" wide, for column 8
(10 for block A and 10 for block B).

Cut 20 segments, 1" wide, for column 10
(10 for block A and 10 for block B).

Cut 20 segments, ¾" wide, for column 12
(10 for block A and 10 for block B).

Cut 16 segments, 1" wide, for column 1
(8 for block C and 8 for block D).

Cut 16 segments, 1" wide, for column 9
(8 for block C and 8 for block D).

Cut 16 segments, 2½" wide, for column 11
(8 for block C and 8 for block D).

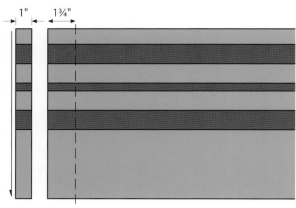

Strip set 3. Make 4.

Cut 20 segments, 1¾" wide, for column 3
  (10 for block A and 10 for block B).

Cut 20 segments, 1" wide, for column 5
  (10 for block A and 10 for block B).

Cut 20 segments, 1¾" wide, for column 7
  (10 for block A and 10 for block B).

Cut 16 segments, 1¾" wide, for column 4
  (8 for block C and 8 for block D).

Cut 16 segments, 1¾" wide, for column 6
  (8 for block C and 8 for block D).

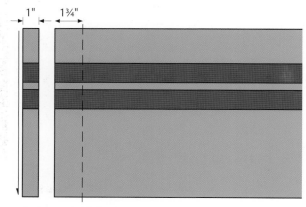

Strip set 4. Make 4.

Cut 20 segments, 1¾" wide, for column 4
  (10 for block A and 10 for block B).

Cut 20 segments, 1¾" wide, for column 6
  (10 for block A and 10 for block B).

Cut 16 segments, 1¾" wide, for column 3
  (8 for block C and 8 for block D).

Cut 16 segments, 1" wide, for column 5
  (8 for block C and 8 for block D).

Cut 16 segments, 1¾" wide, for column 7
  (8 for block C and 8 for block D).

Completing the Blocks

1. Using one segment from each strip set as described, make 10 A blocks, sewing the columns in numerical order 1–12 from left to right. Press the seam allowances in one direction as shown.

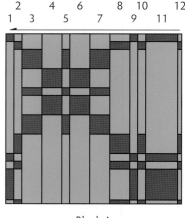

Block A
Make 10.

2. Using one segment from each strip set as described, make 10 B blocks by sewing the columns in reverse order 12–1 from left to right. Press the seam allowances in one direction as shown.

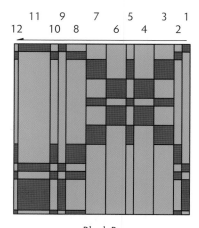

Block B
Make 10.

3. Using one segment from each strip set as described, make eight C blocks, sewing the columns in numerical order 1–12 from left to right. Press the seam allowances in one direction as shown.

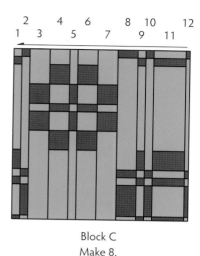

Block C
Make 8.

4. Using one segment from each strip set as described, make eight D blocks by sewing the columns in reverse order 12–1 from left to right. Press the seam allowances in one direction as shown.

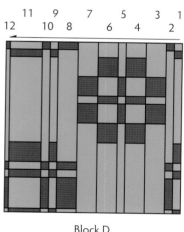

Block D
Make 8.

Assembling the Quilt

1. Arrange the blocks as shown in the quilt assembly diagram below. Note that some of the blocks are rotated 180° to form the quilt pattern.

2. Once your blocks are all arranged, sew them together in rows, pressing the seam allowances in opposite directions from row to row. Then sew the rows together and press the seam allowances in one direction. The quilt-top center should measure 66½" square.

3. Join seven of the black 2½"-wide strips end to end. From the pieced strip, cut two 66½"-long strips and two 70½"-long strips. Sew the 66½"-long strips to opposite sides of the quilt top. Press the seam allowances toward the border. Sew the 70½"-long strips to the top and bottom of the quilt top. Press the seam allowances toward the border.

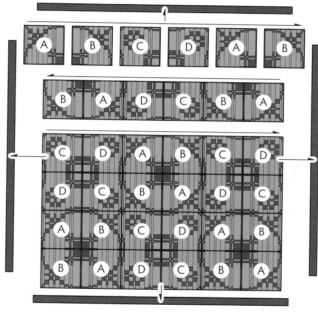

Quilt assembly

Finishing the Quilt

For details on any of the following steps, go to ShopMartingale.com/HowtoQuilt for free downloadable information.

1. Cut and piece the backing fabric and then layer the quilt top with batting and backing.

2. After basting the layers together, hand or machine quilt as desired. Trim the batting and backing so that the edges are even with the quilt top.

3. Using the remaining black 2½"-wide strips, make and attach binding.

Double Compass

Pieced by Fay Ann Grider, Gulph Mills, Pennsylvania, 2012. Quilted by Carol Lee Heisler, Lorac Designs, East Norriton, Pennsylvania.

Quilt size: 43½" x 43½"
Block size: 9¾" x 9¾"

"This quilt is one of the most intriguing of the coverlet-inspired quilts. The Double Compass coverlet gets its name from the circle-in-a-circle design, but you'll also see squares in the center and along the sides, small squares on point, and a large square on point that surrounds the circles. With all this, you would think it would be the most complicated project to construct, but surprisingly it isn't. There are multiple repeats among the columns, and you need only four different strip-set designs to make the entire quilt!

Materials

Yardage is based on 42"-wide fabric.
2⅝ yards of aqua print for blocks
2 yards of purple print for blocks, border, and binding
2½ yards of fabric for backing
47" x 47" piece of batting

Cutting

From the purple print, cut:
21 strips, 1" x 42"
11 strips, 1½" x 42"
3 strips, ¾" x 42"
10 strips, 2½" x 42"

From the aqua print, cut:
5 strips, 1½" x 42"
3 strips, 3½" x 42"
10 strips, 2" x 42"
4 strips, 1" x 42"
4 strips, 3" x 42"
2 strips, ¾" x 42"
2 strips, 4" x 42"
2 strips, 2½" x 42"
2 strips, 1¼" x 42"
2 strips, 5" x 42"
2 strips, 1¾" x 42"

Assembling the Blocks

"Double Compass" requires eight blocks (A) and eight reverse blocks (B). Each block is made of 15 columns; the columns are simply sewn in reverse order to make the reverse blocks. We'll start by making the strip sets.

Making the Strip Sets

For this quilt, you'll use four different strip-set configurations as described in the table below. Sew the specified strips in order from left to right. Press the seam allowances in one direction. Make three of strip set 1 and two *each* of strip sets 2, 3, and 4.

Strip set number	Strip length	Strip width and color (P=Purple; A=Aqua)								
1	42"	1" P	1½" A	1½" P	3½" A	1" P	2" A	1" P	2" A	¾" P
2	42"	1" A	1½" P	1½" A	1½" P	3" A	1" P	3" A	1" P	¾" A
3	42"	4" A	1½" P	2½" A	1" P	2" A	1" P	1¼" A	—	—
4	42"	5" A	1½" P	2" A	1" P	1" A	1" P	1¾" A	—	—

Cutting the Columns

Cut the strip sets into segments of the specified widths and quantities to assemble blocks A and B. The segment width varies for each strip set, as indicated below.

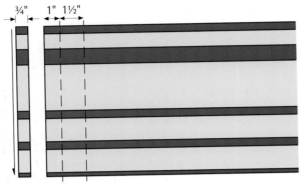

Strip set 1. Make 3.
Cut 16 segments, 1" wide, for column 1
  (8 for block A and 8 for block B).
Cut 16 segments, 1½" wide, for column 3
  (8 for block A and 8 for block B).
Cut 16 segments, 1" wide, for column 7
  (8 for block A and 8 for block B).
Cut 16 segments, 1" wide, for column 11
  (8 for block A and 8 for block B).
Cut 16 segments, ¾" wide, for column 15
  (8 for block A and 8 for block B).

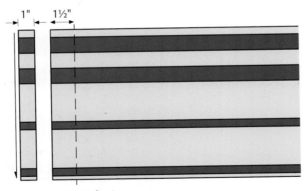

Strip set 2. Make 2.
Cut 16 segments, 1½" wide, for column 2
  (8 for block A and 8 for block B).
Cut 16 segments, 1½" wide, for column 4
  (8 for block A and 8 for block B).
Cut 16 segments, 1" wide, for column 8
  (8 for block A and 8 for block B).
Cut 16 segments, 1" wide, for column 14
  (8 for block A and 8 for block B).

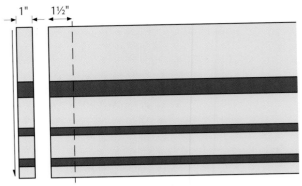

Strip set 3. Make 2.
Cut 16 segments, 1½" wide, for column 5
  (8 for block A and 8 for block B).
Cut 16 segments, 1" wide, for column 9
  (8 for block A and 8 for block B).
Cut 16 segments, 1" wide, for column 13
  (8 for block A and 8 for block B).

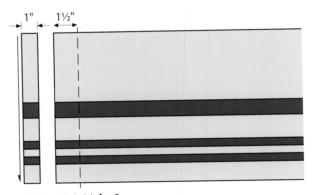

Strip set 4. Make 2.
Cut 16 segments, 1½" wide, for column 6
  (8 for block A and 8 for block B).
Cut 16 segments, 1" wide, for column 10
  (8 for block A and 8 for block B).
Cut 16 segments, 1" wide, for column 12
  (8 for block A and 8 for block B).

Completing the Blocks

1. Using one segment from each strip set as described, make eight A blocks, sewing the columns in numerical order 1–15 from left to right. Press the seam allowances in one direction as shown.

Block A
Make 8.

2. Using one segment from each strip set, make eight B blocks by sewing the columns in reverse order 15–1 from left to right. Press the seam allowances in one direction as shown.

Block B
Make 8.

Assembling the Quilt

1. Arrange the blocks as shown in the quilt assembly diagram above right. Note that some of the blocks are rotated 180° to form the quilt pattern.

2. Once your blocks are all arranged, sew them together in rows, pressing the seam allowances in opposite directions from row to row. Then sew the rows together and press the seam allowances in one direction. The quilt-top center should measure 39½" square.

3. Trim two of the purple 2½"-wide strips to 39½" long and sew them to opposite sides of the quilt top. Press the seam allowances toward the border. Join three of the purple 2½"-wide strips end to end. From the pieced strip, cut two 43½"-long strips and sew them to the top and bottom of the quilt top. Press the seam allowances toward the border.

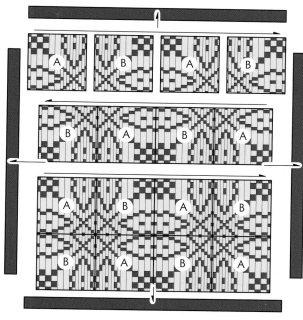

Quilt assembly

Finishing the Quilt

For details on any of the following steps, go to ShopMartingale.com/HowtoQuilt for free downloadable information.

1. Cut and piece the backing fabric and then layer the quilt top with batting and backing.

2. After basting the layers together, hand or machine quilt as desired. Trim the batting and backing so that the edges are even with the quilt top.

3. Using the remaining purple 2½"-wide strips, make and attach binding.

Thirteen States

Pieced and quilted by Carolyn Davis, Morgantown, Pennsylvania, 2012.

Quilt size: 48½" x 48½"
Block size: 5½" x 5½"

> The weaving world is like the quilting world—you never know what's out there until you look. I would have passed right over Thirteen States as just another circle pattern if not for the name. It was intriguing from a historical perspective since it dates back to colonial times. Also, the pattern is just row upon row of circles, so I could find no rhyme or reason for the name. It was intriguing enough that I stopped to look at the circles—and thus discovered a nice pattern. What separates this pattern from most of the other woven coverlets is the size of the block. The quarter-circle block is only 5½", making the entire circle unit 11". This enables you to make a small, multiple-block quilt that shows the circles, curved diamonds, overlapping squares, and rectangles. The block size also makes it suitable for place mats and narrow table runners.

Materials

Yardage is based on 42"-wide fabric.
3¼ yards of orange print for blocks
2½ yards of green print for blocks, border, and binding
3 yards of fabric for backing
52" x 52" piece of batting

Cutting

From the green print, cut:
11 strips, ¾" x 42"
28 strips, 1" x 42"
10 strips, 1½" x 42"
11 strips, 2½" x 42"

From the orange print, cut:
9 strips, 2" x 42"
5 strips, 3" x 42"
11 strips, ¾" x 42"
6 strips, 3½" x 42"
10 strips, 1" x 42"
4 strips, 1¼" x 42"
4 strips, 2¼" x 42"
4 strips, 1¾" x 42"
4 strips, 3¼" x 42"

Assembling the Blocks

"Thirteen States" requires 32 blocks (A) and 32 reverse blocks (B). Each block is made of 10 columns; the columns are simply sewn in reverse order to make the reverse blocks. Since there are multiple repeats among the columns, you only need four different types of strip sets. We'll start by making the strip sets.

Making the Strip Sets

For this quilt, you'll use four different strip-set configurations as described in the table on page 70. Sew the specified strips in order from left to right. Press the seam allowances in one direction. Make five of strip set 1, six of strip set 2, and four *each* of strip sets 3 and 4.

Strip set number	Strip length	Strip width and color (G=Green; O=Orange)					
1	42"	¾" G	2" O	1" G	3" O	1" G	¾" O
2	42"	¾" O	1" G	3½" O	1½" G	1" O	¾" G
3	42"	1¼" O	1" G	2" O	1½" G	2¼" O	—
4	42"	1¾" O	1" G	1" O	1" G	3¼" O	—

Cutting the Columns

Cut the strip sets into segments of the specified widths and quantities to assemble blocks A and B. The segment width varies for each strip set, as indicated below.

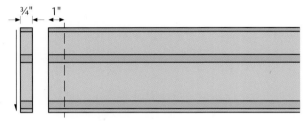

Strip set 1. Make 5.
Cut 64 segments, ¾" wide, for column 1
    (32 for block A and 32 for block B).
Cut 64 segments, 1" wide, for column 5
    (32 for block A and 32 for block B).
Cut 64 segments, 1" wide, for column 9
    (32 for block A and 32 for block B).

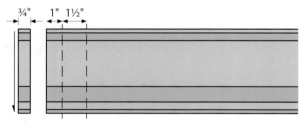

Strip set 2. Make 6.
Cut 64 segments, 1" wide, for column 2
    (32 for block A and 32 for block B).
Cut 64 segments, 1½" wide, for column 8
    (32 for block A and 32 for block B).
Cut 64 segments, ¾" wide, for column 10
    (32 for block A and 32 for block B).

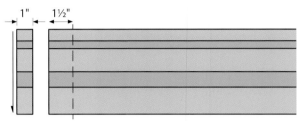

Strip set 3. Make 4.
Cut 64 segments, 1" wide, for column 3
    (32 for block A and 32 for block B).
Cut 64 segments, 1½" wide, for column 7
    (32 for block A and 32 for block B).

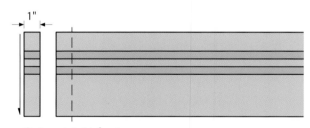

Strip set 4. Make 4.
Cut 64 segments, 1" wide, for column 4
    (32 for block A and 32 for block B).
Cut 64 segments, 1" wide, for column 6
    (32 for block A and 32 for block B).

Completing the Blocks

1. Using one segment from each strip set as described, make 32 A blocks, sewing the columns in numerical order 1–10 from left to right. Press the seam allowances in one direction as shown.

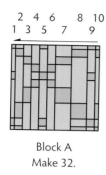

Block A
Make 32.

2. Using one segment from each strip set, make 32 B blocks by sewing the columns in reverse order 10–1 from left to right. Press the seam allowances in one direction as shown.

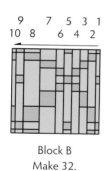

Block B
Make 32.

Assembling the Quilt

1. Arrange the blocks as shown in the quilt assembly diagram above right. Note that some of the blocks are rotated 180° to form the quilt pattern.

2. Once your blocks are all arranged, sew them together in rows, pressing the seam allowances in opposite directions from row to row. Then sew the rows together and press the seam allowances in one direction. The quilt-top center should measure 44½" square.

3. Join the green 2½"-wide strips end to end. From the pieced strip, cut two 44½"-long strips and two 48½"-long strips. Sew the 44½"-long strips to opposite sides of the quilt top. Press the seam allowances toward the border. Sew the 48½"-long strips to the top and bottom of the quilt top. Press the seam allowances toward the border.

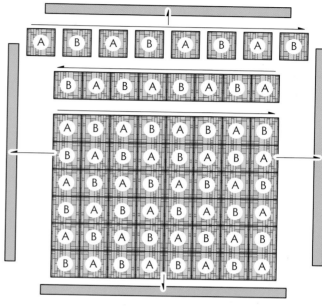

Quilt assembly

Finishing the Quilt

For details on any of the following steps, go to ShopMartingale.com/HowtoQuilt for free downloadable information.

1. Cut and piece the backing fabric and then layer the quilt top with batting and backing.

2. After basting the layers together, hand or machine quilt as desired. Trim the batting and backing so that the edges are even with the quilt top.

3. Using the remaining green 2½"-wide strips, make and attach binding.

Kathy's Star

Pieced and quilted by Robin McMillen, Downingtown, Pennsylvania, 2012.

Quilt size: 49½" x 49½"
Block size: 7½" x 7½"

> "For the longest time I thought that the only motifs in woven coverlets were circles in various configurations—which was fine with me. I merrily went about converting each coverlet design into a quilt. And then we went to Williamsburg, Virginia, where I saw a special exhibit of woven coverlets along with a book, *American Star Work Coverlets*, by Judith Gordon (Design Books, 1995). This publication was full of coverlets featuring stars of all types and in a variety of configurations—enough to make an entire book. When Kathleen, my wife and color consultant, found that I had named a quilt after each of our granddaughters and our daughter, she took a modicum of umbrage, so this one is named for her. When she swapped quilts with our daughter, Robin, I fleetingly thought of renaming the quilt, but self-preservation prevailed and I left it alone."

Materials

Yardage is based on 42"-wide fabric.
2⅝ yards of red print for blocks, border, and binding
1¾ yards of yellow print for blocks
1¼ yards of green print for blocks
⅝ yard of orange print for blocks
3⅛ yards of fabric for backing
53" x 53" piece of batting

Cutting

From the green print, cut:
7 strips, ¾" x 42"
2 strips, 3" x 42"
10 strips, 1" x 42"
1 strip, 3¼" x 42"
1 strip, 2¾" x 42"
1 strip, 2¼" x 42"
1 strip, 1¾" x 42"
1 strip, 1½" x 42"
1 strip, 1¼" x 42"
1 strip, 2½" x 42"

From the yellow print, cut:
2 strips, 2½" x 42"
1 strip, 1½" x 42"
11 strips, 2" x 42"
4 strips, 1" x 42"
2 strips, 1¾" x 42"
2 strips, 1¼" x 42"

9 strips, ¾" x 42"
1 strip, 4¾" x 42"
1 strip, 5½" x 42"

From the orange print, cut:
3 strips, 1½" x 42"
8 strips, 1" x 42"
2 strips, 1¼" x 42"
4 strips, ¾" x 42"

From the red print: cut:
2 strips, 1" x 42"
2 strips, 1½" x 42"
2 strips, 2" x 42"
13 strips, 2½" x 42"
2 strips, 3" x 42"
3 strips, 3½" x 42"
6 strips, 4½" x 42"

Assembling the Blocks

"Kathy's Star" requires 18 blocks (A) and 18 reverse blocks (B). Each block is made of 16 columns; the columns are simply sewn in reverse order to make the reverse blocks. We'll start by making the strip sets.

Making the Strip Sets

For this quilt, you'll make 16 strip sets, each in a different configuration as described in the table on page 74. Sew the specified strips in order, from left to right. Press the seam allowances in one direction.

Strip set number	Strip length	Strip width and color (R=Red; Y=Yellow; O=Orange; G=Green)							
1	42"	¾" G	1½" O	3" G	2½" Y	1" G	1½" O	¾" G	—
2	42"	1" O	3¼" G	1½" Y	1" R	2" Y	1" G	1¼" O	—
3	42"	¾" O	3" G	2" Y	1½" R	2" Y	1" G	¾" O	—
4	42"	2¾" G	2½" Y	2" R	2" Y	¾" G	—	—	—
5	42"	2¼" G	2" Y	1" G	1" Y	2½" R	1¾" Y	—	—
6	42"	1¾" G	2" Y	1½" G	1" Y	3" R	1¼" Y	—	—
7	42"	1¼" G	2" Y	1" G	1" O	1" G	1" Y	3½" R	¾" Y
8	42"	¾" G	2" Y	2½" G	1" Y	3½" R	¾" Y	—	—
9	42"	4¾" Y	3½" R	¾" Y	—	—	—	—	—
10	42"	¾" Y	4½" R	1" O	3" R	¾" Y	—	—	—
11	42"	1¼" Y	4½" R	1" O	2½" R	¾" Y	—	—	—
12	42"	1¾" Y	4½" R	1" O	2" R	¾" Y	—	—	—
13	42"	¾" G	2" Y	4½" R	1" O	1½" R	¾" Y	—	—
14	42"	¾" O	1" G	2" Y	4½" R	1" O	1" R	¾" Y	—
15	42"	1¼" O	1" G	2" Y	4½" R	1" O	¾" G	—	—
16	42"	¾" G	1½" O	1" G	5½" Y	1" G	¾" O	—	—

Cutting the Columns

Cut the strip sets into segments of the specified widths to assemble the blocks. The segment width varies for each strip set, as indicated below. From each strip set, cut 36 segments, 18 for block A and 18 for block B.

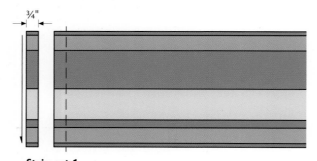

Strip set 1.
Cut 36 segments, ¾" wide, for column 1.

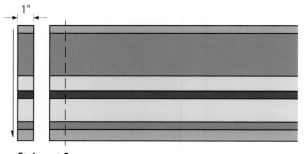

Strip set 2.
Cut 36 segments, 1" wide, for column 2.

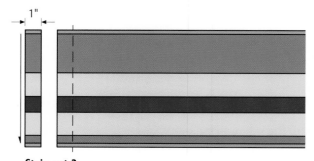

Strip set 3.
Cut 36 segments, 1" wide, for column 3.

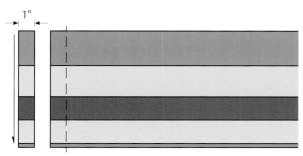

Strip set 4.
Cut 36 segments, 1" wide, for column 4.

Strip set 5.
Cut 36 segments, 1" wide, for column 5.

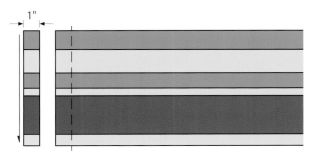

Strip set 6.
Cut 36 segments, 1" wide, for column 6.

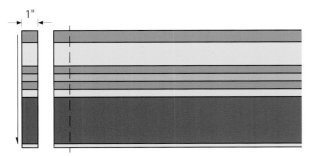

Strip set 7.
Cut 36 segments, 1" wide, for column 7.

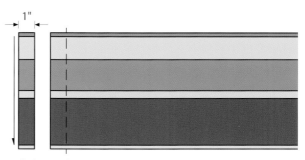

Strip set 8.
Cut 36 segments, 1" wide, for column 8.

Strip set 9.
Cut 36 segments, 1" wide, for column 9.

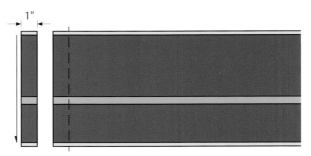

Strip set 10.
Cut 36 segments, 1" wide, for column 10.

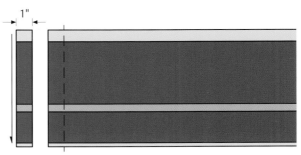

Strip set 11.
Cut 36 segments, 1" wide, for column 11.

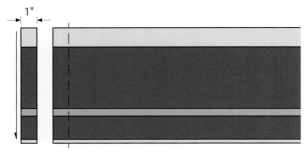

Strip set 12.
Cut 36 segments, 1" wide, for column 12.

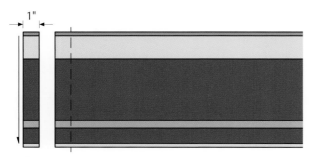

Strip set 13.
Cut 36 segments, 1" wide, for column 13.

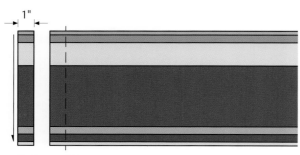

Strip set 14.
Cut 36 segments, 1" wide, for column 14.

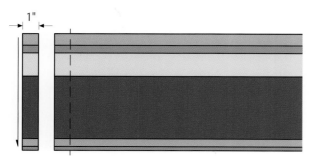

Strip set 15.
Cut 36 segments, 1" wide, for column 15.

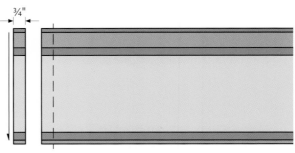

Strip set 16.
Cut 36 segments, ¾" wide, for column 16.

Completing the Blocks

1. Using one segment from each strip set as described, make 18 A blocks, sewing the columns in numerical order 1–16 from left to right. Press the seam allowances in one direction as shown.

Block A
Make 18.

2. Using one segment from each strip set, make 18 B blocks by sewing the columns in reverse order 16–1 from left to right. Press the seam allowances in one direction as shown.

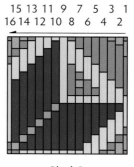

Block B
Make 18.

Assembling the Quilt

1. Arrange the blocks as shown in the quilt assembly diagram below. Note that some of the blocks are rotated 180° to form the quilt pattern.

2. Once your blocks are all arranged, sew them together in rows, pressing the seam allowances in opposite directions from row to row. Then sew the rows together and press the seam allowances in one direction. The quilt-top center should measure 45½" square.

3. Join five of the red 2½"-wide strips end to end. From the pieced strip, cut two 45½"-long strips and two 49½"-long strips. Sew the 45½"-long strips to opposite sides of the quilt top. Press the seam allowances toward the border. Sew the 49½"-long strips to the top and bottom of the quilt top. Press the seam allowances toward the border.

Finishing the Quilt

For details on any of the following steps, go to ShopMartingale.com/HowtoQuilt for free downloadable information.

1. Cut and piece the backing fabric and then layer the quilt top with batting and backing.

2. After basting the layers together, hand or machine quilt as desired. Trim the batting and backing so that the edges are even with the quilt top.

3. Using the remaining red 2½"-wide strips, make and attach binding.

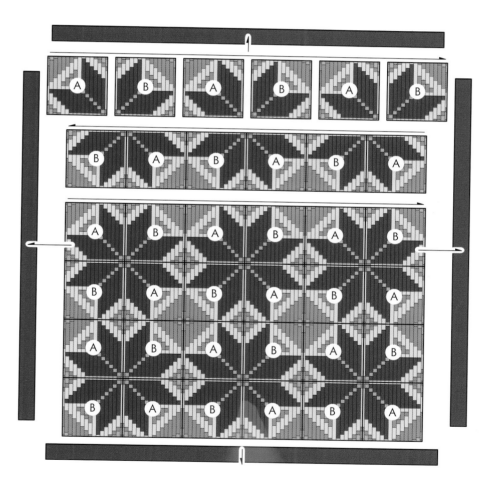

Quilt assembly

Robin's Butterfly

Pieced and quilted by Roberta Lodi, Downingtown, Pennsylvania, 2012.

Quilt size: 37½" x 37½"
Block size: 8¼" x 8¼"

My quest for woven coverlets began at a local museum where I was selling my quilts. The first coverlet that I saw was composed of circles and ovals, and the search was on. Butterfly was the first nonstandard geometric-shape woven coverlet that I found. My daughter, Robin, immediately sprang to mind—elegant, complex, intricate, floats like a butterfly and stings like a bee. Thus the name, "Robin's Butterfly." I originally created a black-and-yellow color scheme, which was truly stunning. Here, quiltmaker Roberta maintained the graphic complexity even though she toned down the colors a bit, using two shades of blue.

Materials

Yardage is based on 42"-wide fabric.

2 yards of light-blue print for blocks

1⅝ yards of dark-blue print for blocks, border, and binding

2⅜ yards of fabric for backing*

41" x 41" piece of batting

If backing fabric is 42" wide after washing, you can use a single width of 1¼ yards.

Cutting

From the dark-blue print, cut:

6 strips, 1" x 42"; cut *2 of the strips into 4 strips, 1" x 21"* (1 will be extra)

6 strips, 1½" x 42"; cut *1 of the strips into 2 strips, 1½" x 21"*

1 strip, 1¾" x 42"

5 strips, 2" x 42"; cut *1 of the strips into 2 strips, 2" x 21"*

2 strips, 1¼" x 42"

5 strip, 2½" x 42"; cut *1 of the strips into 2 strips, 2½" x 21"* (1 will be extra)

2 strips, 2½" x 33½"

2 strips, 2½" x 37½"

From the light-blue print, cut:

3 strips, 1½" x 42"; cut *1 of the strips into 2 strips, 1½" x 21"* (1 will be extra)

2 strips, 3½" x 42"; cut *1 of the strips into 2 strips, 3½" x 21"* (1 will be extra)

4 strips, 2" x 42"; cut *1 of the strips into 2 strips, 2" x 21"* (1 will be extra)

1 strip, ¾" x 42"; cut into 2 strips, ¾" x 21"

2 strips, 4" x 42"; cut *1 of the strips into 2 strips, 4" x 21"* (1 will be extra)

2 strips, 1" x 42"; cut *1 of the strips into 2 strips, 1" x 21"*

3 strips, 2½" x 42"; cut *1 of the strips into 2 strips, 2½" x 21"* (1 will be extra)

1 strip, 4¼" x 42"; cut into 2 strips, 4¼" x 21" (1 will be extra)

2 strips, 1¼" x 42"

3 strips, 3" x 42"

1 strip, 4½" x 42"

1 strip, 3¾" x 42"

Assembling the Blocks

"Robin's Butterfly" requires four blocks (A) and 4 reverse blocks (B). You also need four blocks (C) and four reverse blocks (D). Each block is made of 10 columns; the columns are simply sewn in reverse order to make the reverse blocks. We'll start by making the strip sets.

Making the Strip Sets

For this quilt, you'll make five different strip-set configurations (1–5) for blocks A and B and four different strip-set configurations (6–9) for blocks C and D. Sew the specified strips in order from left to right. Press the seam allowances in one direction.

Design Option

Even if you don't like butterflies, the butterfly block can still work for you. For most of the woven-coverlet quilts, you create a different quilt when the blocks are rotated. In most cases, the new quilt design is clearly reminiscent of the original. That's not the case for the butterfly block. When the blocks are rotated, the butterfly disappears and you create a design reminiscent of a Trip Around the World or Log Cabin Barn Raising quilt.

Strip set number	Strip length	Strip width and color (DB=Dark blue; LB=Light blue)						
1	42"	1" DB	1½" LB	1½" DB	3½" LB	1¾" DB	2" LB	—
2	21"	¾" LB	1" DB	2" LB	1½" DB	4" LB	2" DB	—
3	21"	1" LB	1" DB	2½" LB	2" DB	4¼" LB	—	—
4	42"	1¼" LB	1½" DB	3" LB	2" DB	3" LB	—	—
5	42"	1¼" DB	2" LB	1½" DB	4" LB	2" DB	—	—
6	42"	1¼" LB	1" DB	2" LB	1½" DB	4½" LB	1" DB	—
7	42"	1½" LB	1" DB	2½" LB	2" DB	3¾" LB	—	—
8	42"	1¼" DB	1" LB	1½" DB	3" LB	2" DB	2½" LB	—
9	21"	1" LB	1" DB	1½" LB	1½" DB	3½" LB	2½" DB	¾" LB

Cutting the Columns

Cut the strip sets into segments of the specified widths and quantities to assemble blocks A, B, C, and D. The segment width varies for each strip set, as indicated in each illustration.

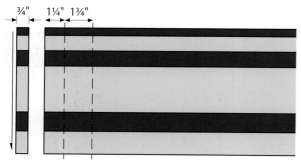

Strip set 1.
Cut 8 segments, ¾" wide, for column 1
  (4 for block A and 4 for block B).
Cut 8 segments, 1¼" wide, for column 5
  (4 for block A and 4 for block B).
Cut 8 segments, 1¾" wide, for column 9
  (4 for block A and 4 for block B).

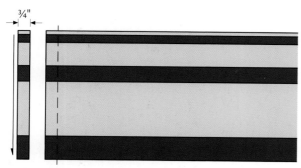

Strip set 2.
Cut 8 segments, ¾" wide, for column 2
  (4 for block A and 4 for block B).

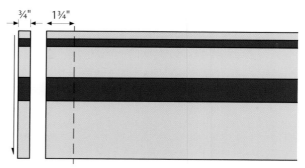

Strip set 3.
Cut 8 segments, ¾" wide, for column 3
  (4 for block A and 4 for block B).
Cut 8 segments, 1¾" wide, for column 7
  (4 for block A and 4 for block B).

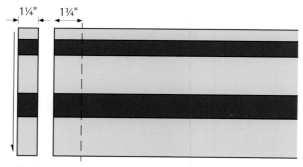

Strip set 4.
Cut 8 segments, 1¼" wide, for column 4
  (4 for block A and 4 for block B).
Cut 8 segments, 1¾" wide, for column 8
  (4 for block A and 4 for block B).

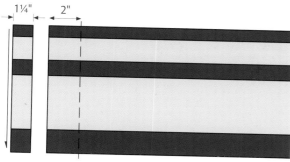

Strip set 5.
Cut 8 segments, 1¼" wide, for column 6
  (4 for block A and 4 for block B).
Cut 8 segments, 2" wide, for column 10
  (4 for block A and 4 for block B).

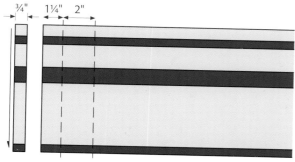

Strip set 6.
Cut 8 segments, 2" wide, for column 1
  (4 for block C and 4 for block D).
Cut 8 segments, 1¼" wide, for column 5
  (4 for block C and 4 for block D).
Cut 8 segments, ¾" wide, for column 9
  (4 for block C and 4 for block D).

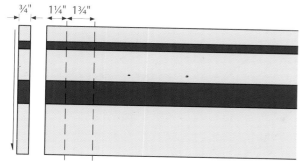

Strip set 7.
Cut 8 segments, 1¾" wide, for column 2
  (4 for block C and 4 for block D).
Cut 8 segments, 1¼" wide, for column 6
  (4 for block C and 4 for block D).
Cut 8 segments, ¾" wide, for column 10
  (4 for block C and 4 for block D).

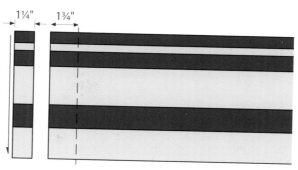

Strip set 8.
Cut 8 segments, 1¾" wide, for column 3
  (4 for block C and 4 for block D).
Cut 8 segments, 1¼" wide, for column 7
  (4 for block C and 4 for block D).

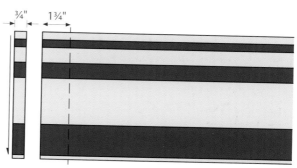

Strip set 9.
Cut 8 segments, 1¾" wide, for column 4
  (4 for block C and 4 for block D).
Cut 8 segments, ¾" wide, for column 8
  (4 for block C and 4 for block D).

Completing the Blocks

1. Using the segments from strip sets 1–5 as described, make four A blocks, sewing the columns in numerical order 1–10 from left to right. Press the seam allowances in one direction as shown.

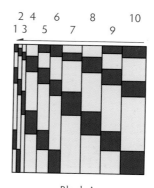

Block A
Make 4.

2. Using the segments from strip sets 1–5 as described, make four B blocks by sewing the columns in reverse order 10–1 from left to right. Press the seam allowances in one direction as shown.

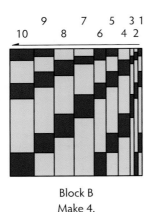

Block B
Make 4.

3. Using the segments from strip sets 6–9 as described, make four C blocks, sewing the columns in numerical order 1–10 from left to right. Press the seam allowances in one direction as shown.

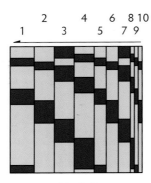

Block C
Make 4.

4. Using the segments from strip sets 6–9 as described, make four D blocks by sewing the columns in reverse order 10–1 from left to right. Press the seam allowances in one direction as shown.

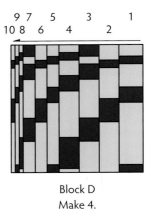

Block D
Make 4.

Assembling the Quilt

1. Arrange the blocks as shown in the quilt assembly diagram on page 83. Note that some of the blocks are rotated 180° to form the quilt pattern.

2. Once your blocks are all arranged, sew them together in rows, pressing the seam allowances in opposite directions from row to row. Then sew the rows together and press the seam allowances in one direction. The quilt-top center should measure 33½" square.

3. Sew the dark-blue 33½"-long strips to opposite sides of the quilt top. Press the seam allowances toward the border. Sew the dark-blue 37½"-long strips to the top and bottom of the quilt top. Press the seam allowances toward the border.

Finishing the Quilt

For details on any of the following steps, go to ShopMartingale.com/HowtoQuilt for free downloadable information.

1. Cut and piece the backing fabric and then layer the quilt top with batting and backing.

2. After basting the layers together, hand or machine quilt as desired. Trim the batting and backing so that the edges are even with the quilt top.

3. Using the remaining dark-blue 2½" x 42" strips, make and attach binding.

Quilt assembly

Snowball and Pine Tree

Pieced and quilted by Bob DeCarli, Downingtown, Pennsylvania, 2012.

Quilt size: 47½" x 47½"
Block size: 10¾" x 10¾"

> After discovering a circle-oval coverlet at the Brandywine River Museum in Chadds Ford, Pennsylvania, I found woven coverlets everywhere. But they were mostly of the star, circle, oval, or diamond variety. Finally, in the last pages of a book long since misplaced, I found a photograph of a coverlet with a Snowball and Pine Tree design. This coverlet design opened up a new world for me to explore.

Materials

Yardage is based on 42"-wide fabric.

4 yards of blue print for blocks, border, and binding

1½ yards of white-on-white print for blocks

⅞ yard of green print for blocks

2 yards of fabric for backing

51" x 51" piece of batting

Cutting

From the blue print, cut:

6 strips, ¾" x 42"; cut *5 of the strips* into 10 strips, ¾" x 21" (1 will be extra)

3 strips, 1¾" x 42"; cut into 6 strips, 1¾" x 21" (1 will be extra)

6 strips, 2⅜" x 42"; into 12 strips, 2⅜" x 21"

13 strips, 1⅛" x 42"; cut *11 of the strips* into 22 strips, 1⅛" x 21"

1 strip, 1½" x 42"; cut into 2 strips, 1½" x 21" (1 will be extra)

2 strips, 1⅞" x 42"; cut into 4 strips, 1⅞" x 21"

2 strips, 3" x 42"; cut into 4 strips, 3" x 21" (1 will be extra)

2 strips, 2¼" x 42"; cut into 4 strips, 2¼" x 21" (1 will be extra)

2 strips, 3⅝" x 42"; cut into 4 strips, 3⅝" x 21" (1 will be extra)

2 strips, 2⅝" x 42"; cut into 4 strips, 2⅝" x 21" (1 will be extra)

1 strip, 7" x 42"; cut into 2 strips, 7" x 21" (1 will be extra)

1 strip, 11¼" x 42"; cut into 2 strips, 11¼" x 21" (1 will be extra)

1 strip, 4¼" x 42"

1 strip, 3¼" x 42"; cut into 2 strips, 3¼" x 21" (1 will be extra)

1 strip, 3½" x 42"

1 strip, 7⅝" x 42"

10 strips, 2½" x 42"

From the green print, cut:

2 strips, 2" x 42"; cut into 4 strips, 2" x 21"

2 strips, 2⅜" x 42"; cut into 4 strips, 2⅜" x 21" (1 will be extra)

1 strip, 1⅞" x 42"; cut into 2 strips, 1⅞" x 21" (1 will be extra)

1 strip, 2⅝" x 42"; cut into 2 strips, 2⅝" x 21" (1 will be extra)

2 strips, 1½" x 42"; cut into 4 strips, 1½" x 21" (1 will be extra)

1 strip, 1¾" x 42"; cut into 2 strips, 1¾" x 21" (1 will be extra)

3 strips, 1⅛" x 42"; cut into 6 strips, 1⅛" x 21" (1 will be extra)

2 strips, ¾" x 42"; cut into 4 strips, ¾" x 21" (1 will be extra)

1 strip, 1¼" x 42"; cut into 2 strips, 1¼" x 21" (1 will be extra)

From the white-on-white print, cut:

17 strips, 1⅛" x 42"; cut *16 of the strips* into 32 strips, 1⅛" x 21"

4 strips, ¾" x 42"; cut *3 of the strips* into 6 strips, ¾" x 21"

2 strips, 1¾" x 42"; cut into 4 strips, 1¾" x 21"

2 strips, 2" x 42"; cut *1 of the strips* into 2 strips, 2" x 21"

7 strips, 2⅜" x 42"; cut *5 of the strips* into 10 strips, 2⅜" x 21"

Assembling the Blocks

"Snowball and Pine Tree" requires eight blocks (A) and eight reverse blocks (B). Each block is made of 19 columns; the columns are simply sewn in reverse order to make the reverse blocks. We'll start by making the strip sets.

Making the Strip Sets

For this quilt, there is only one repeat among the columns, so you'll make 18 different strip-set configurations. Sew the specified strips in order, from left to right. Press the seam allowances in one direction.

Strip set number	Strip length	Strip width and color (B=Blue; G=Green; W=White)										
1	21"	¾" B	2" G	1¾" B	1⅛" W	2⅜" B	2⅜" G	1⅛" B	2⅜" G	1⅛" B	¾" W	—
2	21"	1⅞" G	1½" B	1⅛" W	1⅛" B	1⅛" W	2⅜" B	2⅜" G	1⅛" B	2⅝" G	—	—
3	21"	1½" G	1⅞" B	1⅛" W	1⅛" B	1⅛" W	3" B	1¾" G	1¾" B	2" G	—	—
4	21"	1⅛" G	2¼" B	1⅛" W	1⅛" B	1⅛" W	3⅝" B	1⅛" G	2⅜" B	1⅛" G	¾" B	—
5	21"	¾" G	2⅝" B	1⅛" W	1⅛" B	1⅛" W	7" B	—	—	—	—	—
6	21"	11¼" B	—	—	—	—	—	—	—	—	—	—
7	42"	¾" B	2" W	4¼" B	2⅜" W	1⅛" B	2⅜" W	1⅛" B	¾" W	—	—	—
8	21"	¾" W	3¼" B	1⅛" W	1⅛" B	1¾" W	2⅜" B	1⅛" W	2⅜" B	1⅛" W	¾" B	—
9	42"	3½" B	1⅛" W	7⅝" B	—	—	—	—	—	—	—	—
10	21"	¾" G	2⅝" B	1⅛" W	1⅛" B	1⅛" W	3⅝" B	1⅛" W	2⅜" B	1⅛" W	¾" B	—
11	21"	1⅛" G	2¼" B	1⅛" W	1⅛" B	1⅛" W	3" B	1¾" W	1¾" B	2" W	—	—
12	21"	1½" G	1⅞" B	1⅛" W	1⅛" B	1⅛" W	2⅜" B	2⅜" W	1⅛" B	2⅜" W	¾" B	—
13	21"	¾" B	2" G	1¾" B	1⅛" W	2⅜" B	2⅜" W	1⅛" B	2⅜" W	1⅛" B	¾" W	—
14	21"	¾" G	2⅝" B	1⅛" W	1⅛" B	1⅛" W	3⅝" B	1⅛" W	2⅜" B	1⅛" W	¾" B	—
15	21"	1⅛" G	2¼" B	1⅛" W	1⅛" B	1⅛" W	3" B	1¾" W	1¾" B	2" W	—	—
16	21"	1½" G	1⅞" B	1⅛" W	1⅛" B	1⅛" W	2⅜" B	2⅜" W	1⅛" B	2⅜" W	¾" B	—
17	21"	¾" B	2" G	1¾" B	1⅛" W	2⅜" B	2⅜" W	1⅛" B	2⅜" W	1⅛" B	¾" W	—
18	21"	¾" W	1¼" G	1⅞" B	1⅛" W	1⅛" B	1⅛" W	2⅜" B	2⅜" W	1⅛" B	2⅜" W	¾" B

Cutting the Columns

Cut the strip sets into segments of the specified widths to assemble the blocks. The segment width varies for each strip set, as indicated below. From each strip set (except strip set 7), cut 16 segments, 8 for block A and 8 for block B. From strip set 7, cut 32 segments, 16 for block A and 16 for block B.

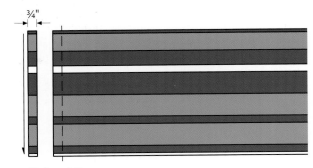

Strip set 1.
Cut 16 segments, ¾" wide, for column 1.

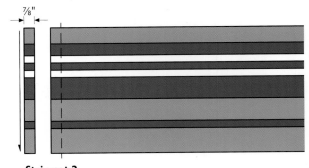

Strip set 2.
Cut 16 segments, ⅞" wide, for column 2.

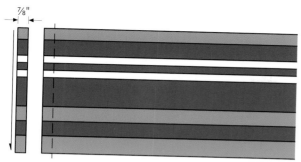

Strip set 3.
Cut 16 segments, ⅞" wide, for column 3.

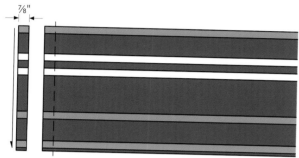

Strip set 4.
Cut 16 segments, ⅞" wide, for column 4.

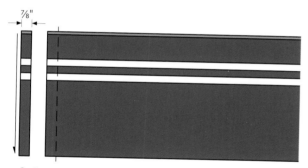

Strip set 5.
Cut 16 segments, ⅞" wide, for column 5.

Strip set 6.
Cut 16 segments, 1⅛" wide, for column 6.

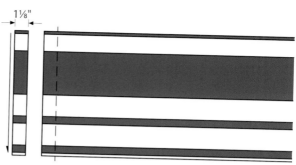

Strip set 7.
Cut 32 segments, 1⅛" wide, for columns 7 and 9.

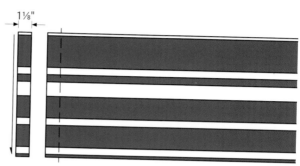

Strip set 8.
Cut 16 segments, 1⅛" wide, for column 8.

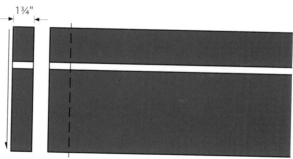

Strip set 9.
Cut 16 segments, 1¾" wide, for column 10.

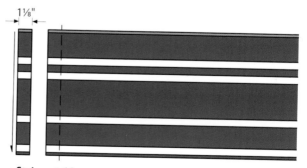

Strip set 10.
Cut 16 segments, 1⅛" wide, for column 11.

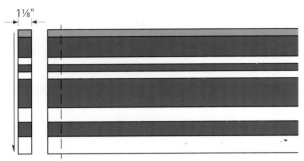

Strip set 11.
Cut 16 segments, 1⅛" wide, for column 12.

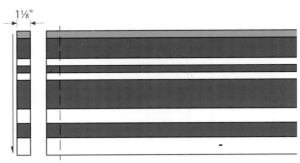

Strip set 15.
Cut 16 segments, 1⅛" wide, for column 16.

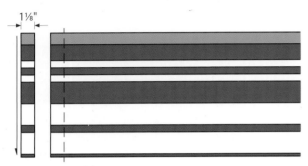

Strip set 12.
Cut 16 segments, 1⅛" wide, for column 13.

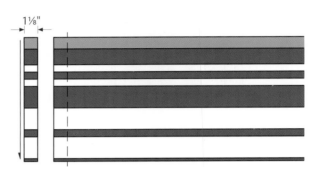

Strip set 16.
Cut 16 segments, 1⅛" wide, for column 17.

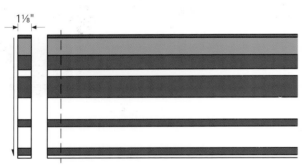

Strip set 13.
Cut 16 segments, 1⅛" wide, for column 14.

Strip set 17.
Cut 16 segments, 1⅛" wide, for column 18.

Strip set 14.
Cut 16 segments, 1⅛" wide, for column 15.

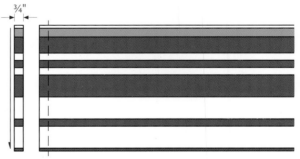

Strip set 18.
Cut 16 segments, ¾" wide, for column 19.

Completing the Blocks

1. Using one segment from each strip set as described, make eight A blocks, sewing the columns in numerical order 1–19 from left to right. Press the seam allowances in one direction as shown.

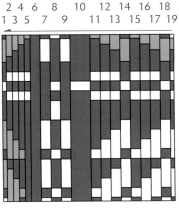

Block A
Make 8.

2. Using one segment from each strip set, make eight B blocks by sewing the columns in reverse order 19–1 from left to right. Press the seam allowances in one direction as shown.

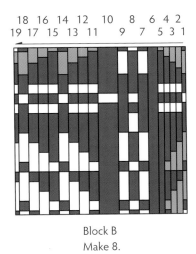

Block B
Make 8.

Assembling the Quilt

1. Arrange the blocks as shown in the quilt assembly diagram above right. Note that some of the blocks are rotated 180° to form the quilt pattern.

2. Once your blocks are all arranged, sew them together in rows, pressing the seam allowances in opposite directions from row to row. Then sew the rows together and press the seam allowances in one direction. The quilt-top center should measure 43½" square.

3. Join five of the blue 2½"-wide strips end to end. From the pieced strip, cut two 43½"-long strips and two 47½"-long strips. Sew the 43½"-long strips to opposite sides of the quilt top. Press the seam allowances toward the border. Sew the 47½"-long strips to the top and bottom of the quilt top. Press the seam allowances toward the border.

Quilt assembly

Finishing the Quilt

For details on any of the following steps, go to ShopMartingale.com/HowtoQuilt for free downloadable information.

1. Cut and piece the backing fabric and then layer the quilt top with batting and backing.

2. After basting the layers together, hand or machine quilt as desired. Trim the batting and backing so that the edges are even with the quilt top.

3. Using the remaining blue 2½"-wide strips, make and attach binding.

Variations on a Theme

"The world of woven coverlets offers a seemingly unlimited number of possible quilt designs, using stars, circles, butterflies, flowers, squares, and combinations of the different shapes. But it's even better than that. You can create designs with the weaving blocks that you can't construct in the weaving world. Weaving appears to be somewhat static; you weave the same for every row so that you keep creating circles or squares or whatever the pattern may be. You can't make half circles or three-quarter circles or any other variation— you can only make circles.

Quilt blocks are not as restrictive. You can rotate any block any number of times and pair it with other blocks. You can change the sizes of the columns to make a new quilt design. You can modify the blocks and create a completely different quilt. You can omit sections of the weaving block and insert other pieced or appliquéd blocks. The variations are too numerous to count. In this section, you'll find 10 variations based on the quilts featured in this book. I'm sure you can dream up even more!"

Twist and Turn

You can twist and turn the blocks for any of the quilts and create a multitude of different quilt designs.

Consider "Ezekiel's Wheel" and start with the quilt layout shown on page 43. You can rotate any block 90° clockwise, 180°, or 90° counterclockwise and create a completely new quilt pattern. Two variations are shown below.

Follow the same process on any of the other "wheel-circle" quilts, including "Sunny South" (page 16) and "Thirteen States" (page 68), to create unique quilts.

If you start with the basic layout for "Charlotte's Garden" (page 37) and rotate each block 180°, you create a "heart-garden" in the center and stars in the corners.

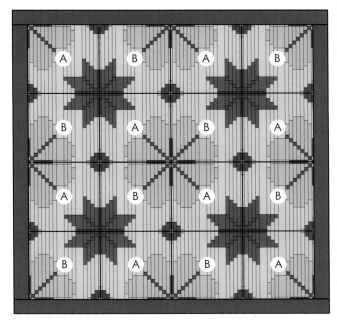

"Charlotte's Garden"
variation

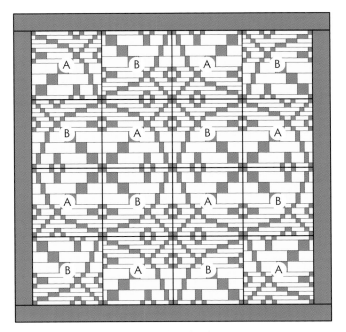

"Ezekiel's Wheel"
variations

If you start with the basic layout for "Miranda's Puzzle" (page 47) and rotate each block 180°, you create a star in the corner and "arrows" pointing toward the center.

Use the two-block quilt layout for "Ludwig's Corner" and rotate each block 180°, and you get a fantastic quilt that looks like no known woven coverlet.

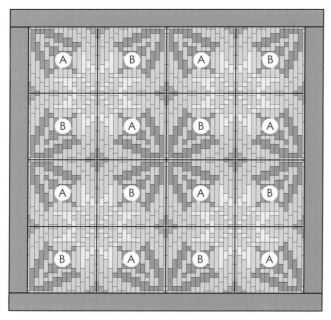

"Miranda's Puzzle"
variation

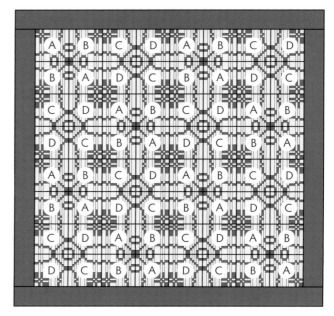

"Ludwig's Corner"
variation

The designs become even more interesting when you look at two-block quilts, especially "Ludwig's Corner" (page 26) and "Red Lion" (page 59). Using the circle block of "Ludwig's Corner" creates a variation of a Wheel quilt, while using just the square block yields an extraordinary design that looks nothing like the original quilt.

If you start with the quilt layout for "Red Lion" and rotate each block 180°, you'll see that the circles and squares disappear, replaced by diamonds with loops on the points.

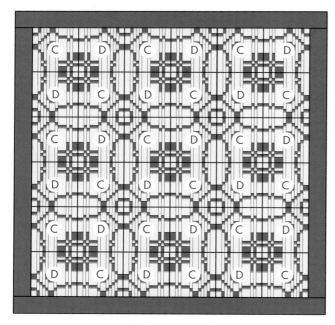

"Ludwig's Corner"
using the square blocks only

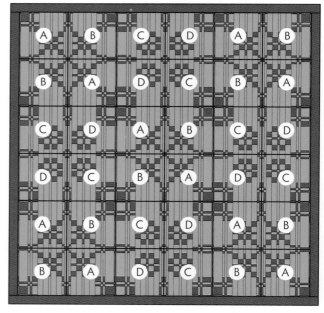

"Red Lion"
variation

Block Modifications

At the risk of sounding like a high school math teacher (which I was in a previous life), I have to mention the extensive number of quilts you can make from just the basic set of weaving blocks. This is doubled or tripled when you toss in the twisting and turning. The number goes toward infinity when you start *modifying* the blocks.

Circles in Circles

The circle-wheel blocks are the easiest to modify. Using the block in "Ezekiel's Wheel" (page 43) as an example, replace some of the dark pieces in the upper-left corner with light pieces, and insert some colored pieces and additional dark pieces along the arc of the circle. This creates a circle-in-a-circle design that is strikingly different from the original version. You can make similar modifications to the other circle-type blocks, namely those featured in "Sunny South" (page 16), "Wedding Ring" (page 20), "Ludwig's Corner" (page 26), "Double Compass" (page 64), and "Thirteen States" (page 68).

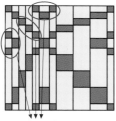 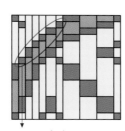

Delete dark pieces.   Insert dark pieces.

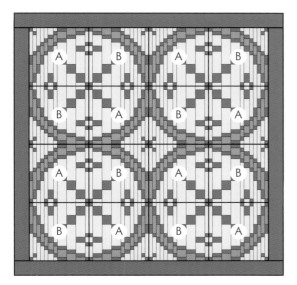

"Ezekiel's Wheel"
modified design

Beyond Circles

As a mathematician, I am forever enchanted by circles, but I suspect this is not the case for most of the rest of the world. Fortunately, the circles in the weaving blocks are very accommodating in that they can easily be transformed into ovals. Consider the block in "Thirteen States" (page 68) You can double the column widths to create a block with an oval arc instead of a circle, which results in oval shapes across the quilt top. The oval block design is great for place mats and table runners. You can make similar modifications to the other circle blocks featured throughout the book.

 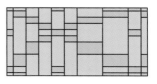

Circle block   Oval block

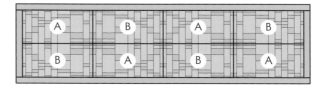

"Thirteen States"
variation

Windows

My wife, Kathleen, likes to appliqué. She watched patiently as I made the quilts and drafted the outline for this book. She worked quietly on a quilt with appliquéd birds, giving no notice to the piecing world, until one day when she looked up and said, "Can't you use the weaving blocks to do appliqué?" This gave rise to another modification—windows. You replace sections of the weaving block with other pieced or appliquéd blocks. This works for all the weaving blocks, but is especially easy with the circle blocks. Using the block from "Ezekiel's Wheel" (page 43) as an example, remove a small square section from the upper-left corner and a larger square section from the bottom-right corner. Separate the block along the seam lines to make square (or rectangular) sections. Replace the sections with plain squares for appliqué, or use pieced squares instead. When you lay out four blocks in rows of two blocks each, you create a large square (or block) in the center and small squares in the corner.

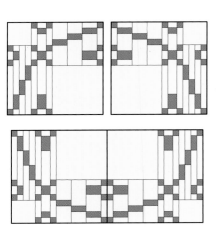

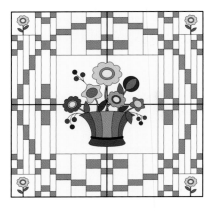

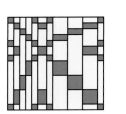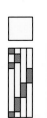

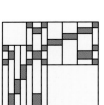

The weaving-quilt world is vast and almost totally unexplored. The options for blocks, variations, and modifications are abundant and inspiring. We have only just begun!

Acknowledgments

I know of no words sufficient to convey my thanks and gratitude to the members of the Penn Oaks Quilt Guild. Without a moment of hesitation, they jumped in and made the most astonishing set of quilts. I will never be able to thank them enough. They are:

Kathleen DeCarli, Downingtown, Pennsylvania—my wife

Robin McMillen, Downingtown, Pennsylvania—my daughter

Ellen McMillen, Downingtown, Pennsylvania—Robin's mother-in-law

Sara Borr, Downingtown, Pennsylvania

Carolyn Davis, Morgantown, Pennsylvania

Jean Fox, West Chester, Pennsylvania

Fay Ann Grider, Gulph Mills, Pennsylvania

Roberta Lodi, Downingtown, Pennsylvania

Kelly Meanix, Downingtown, Pennsylvania

Myrna Paluba, Wayne, Pennsylvania

Pat Sherman, Lancaster, Pennsylvania

Pat Smith, Downingtown, Pennsylvania

Cindy Vognetz, Phoenixville, Pennsylvania

Special thanks to Carol Lee Heisler of Lorac Designs (www.loracdesignsclh.com), East Norriton, Pennsylvania, for quilting several of these quilts.

Left to right, seated: Sara Borr, Roberta Lodi, Myrna Paluba, Jean Fox, Fay Ann Grider;
middle row: Cindy Vognetz, Kathleen DeCarli, Ellen McMillen, Pat Smith;
back row: Kelly Meanix, Robin McMillen, Carolyn Davis, Pat Sherman. (Photo by Bob DeCarli.)

Bob DeCarli's first life was as a math professor at a Catholic girls college in Buffalo, New York. He moved on to function as an engineer at Lockheed Martin in Valley Forge, all the while continuing to teach math at local colleges. In 1992, his wife, Kathleen, asked for help in making a quilt for their daughter's wedding. She showed him how to make a four-patch unit, and he was hooked. As a mathematician, the seemingly endless number of patterns fascinated him. He has designed blocks and quilts since 1993, receiving a ribbon at the Vermont Quilt Festival and a blue ribbon at the Pennsylvania Quilt Extravaganza for "Butterfly."

He discovered Electric Quilt in 2005 (in fact, he used EQ5 to design his prizewinning "Butterfly"), and has since designed more than 1,000 quilts and blocks, including block and quilt settings for his wife's appliqué projects. His primary interest, besides teaching, is designing various sizes of interlocking Log Cabin designs and converting weaving patterns into quilt designs. In each area, the number of possibilities knows no limits, but he pursues them one at a time.

The author in 2004 with his blue-ribbon "Butterfly" quilt